KU-621-704

A Concise Chronology of Typesetting Developments 1886–1986

L. W. Wallis

**The Wynkyn de Worde Society
in association with
Lund Humphries London**

Copyright © 1988 L. W. Wallis

First published in 1988 by
The Wynkyn de Worde Society
in association with
Lund Humphries Publishers Ltd.
16 Pembridge Road, London W11

ISBN 0 85331 538 8
British Library Cataloguing
in Publication Data available

Produced for the publishers by
John Taylor Book Ventures

Typeset by AM International Ltd.
Hemel Hempstead

Printed by Severnside Printers Ltd.
Upton upon Severn

CONTENTS

Preface	*page* v
1886	1
1896	4
1906	8
1916	12
1926	16
1936	21
1946	24
1956	28
1966	36
1976	53
1986	70
Index	76

ACKNOWLEDGEMENTS

This book would never have been published without the support of several people. John Taylor, of the Wynkyn de Worde Society, has been particularly tenacious in pursuing the idea when the softer option would have been to drop it.

Not for the first time I am indebted to Terry Lane, Group Managing Director of AM International Ltd., for permission to set the text on equipment manufactured and owned by that company and for subsidising the production. In this instance, the book has been composed and made-up on an Epics Text Management System and output on a Varityper 6850 phototypesetter. Other colleagues from AM International have generously given their co-operation and production skills. Sandra Wheaton-Rush captured on a Stearns word processing system the original text which Roger Jackson ably transferred and processed through the Epics system and John Newberry helped with many other aspects of the production.

Another old friend, Alan Hughes, proprietor of Severnside Printers Ltd. and a member of the Wynkyn de Worde Society, has undertaken the repro work and printing. He is also closely associated with the subject matter of the book as a pioneer of computer-controlled typesetting in the 1960s when Managing Director of Comprite Ltd.

Many other friends have read through the text and made helpful suggestions: Aaron Burns, John Dreyfus, Brian Mulholland, Arthur Phillips, H. O. (Harry) Smith, and Peter Whittaker. As is customary on these occasions, I admit responsibility for any errors.

L.W.W.

PREFACE

In 1886 Ottmar Mergenthaler completed development of the Blower
Linotype machine which was installed at the *New York Tribune* in
July and worked successfully. It was a momentous landmark in the
evolution of the printing industry. For more than four hundred years
in Europe the composition of type had been accomplished by hand and
in essential technical principle remained unchanged for the whole of
the period. As a labour-intensive process, the speed of hand-setting
was pedestrian reaching not much more than 1,000 ens per hour.
Many inventors were attracted to the task of mechanising the job and
numerous calamitous failures preceded the earliest durable solution to
the problem by Ottmar Mergenthaler. At a rough estimate the number
of composing and distributing machines envisaged before 1886
exceeded a hundred: the first proposal emanating from Dr. William
Church in 1822. Some achieved a measure of effectiveness industrially
as instanced by the Hattersley and Kastenbein which set pre-cast
founders' types. Emergence of the Blower Linotype did not stifle
inventiveness and in the next forty years another two hundred
machines were proposed and a few proved to be outstanding successes
and endured as competitors or complements to the Linotype, such as
the Linograph, Typograph, Monotype, Intertype, and Ludlow.

Remarkably the technical methods embodied in the Blower
Linotype served as the basis for linecasting practice over the next
ninety years until the technique went into commercial decline as
alternative processes matured. Some two hundred Blower Linotype
machines were manufactured totally and approximately sixty of them
entered the United Kingdom. In broad appearance the Blower
Linotype did not look vastly different from linecasters introduced
several decades later, though smaller brass matrices impressed with a
single character were utilised. They circulated individually throughout
the machine and enabled corrections to be made as assembled. The
matrices were stored in vertical metal tubes for release by keyboard
operation on to an inclined chute to be carried laterally by a blast of air
to an assembly point. It was the blast of air which earned the nickname
Blower Linotype. After completion of a line, the composed matrices
were presented to the face of a mould, justified with stepped spaces,
and a slug cast by forcing metal through the mould and into the
depressed images of the matrices. Finally the matrices were lifted to the
top and back of the machine and returned through a distributor
mechanism to the original storage tubes for re-use. Apart from
refinements for convenience of operation, for greater reliability, for
improvement in slug quality, and for extended typographical
flexibility, the practice of linecasting has perpetuated the sound
principles of the Linotype Model 1 machine of 1890 (a direct
descendent of the Blower) ever since.

In the hundred years between 1886 and 1986 the nature of
typesetting has altered radically. As stated previously, the composition
of type had remained a handicraft for a little over four hundred years
and mechanisation of the process occurred rapidly at the turn of the
century with the introduction of Linotype and Monotype equipment
and a little later Intertype and Ludlow systems. However the heyday
of the linecaster in Europe lasted scarcely ninety years before being
unceremoniously dislodged by phototypesetting machines with great
frequency from the late 1960s and to a lesser degree in prior years.
Mechanical composition of metal type had endured as a prime
industrial process for about a quarter of the length of time spanned by
the preceding handicraft era. Phototypesetting machines founded on
image formation from photo-matrices had a pre-eminent period of
hardly twenty-five years prior to ceding dominance to digital CRT
machines which have been at the forefront of technology for about ten
years prior to 1986. Raster imagesetters, using digital founts and often

laser exposure, seem poised to supplant the CRT units. Quite definitely the rate of change quickens to a bewildering degree.

Perhaps one should not be too surprised by the chain of events because as the Blower Linotype reached maturity and successfully mechanised the setting of type, a number of inventors were contemplating and experimenting with alternative methods. In 1887 a proposal was made to build a composing machine yielding reproduction proofs, a concept that underwent a fitful revival with the Typary and Orotype systems of the 1920s and 1930s. As early as 1893 and 1896, a couple of innovative spirits were propounding the application of photography to the setting of type.

In the following pages, a selective collection of events and developments occurring in typesetting over the hundred years between 1886 and 1986 have been recorded. Most of the information has a British and American bias. Little detail has been included, the intention being more to present a broad picture of trends and major happenings. Much has taken place in the period reviewed. It seems incredible to reflect that as the widespread mechanisation of typesetting was about to occur, the typefounders in the USA were meeting in a concerted effort to standardise and to regularise the sizes of metal types and eventually to settle upon the point system. Another important development in the period was the renaissance in type design led by Stanley Morison at the Monotype Corporation Ltd. and by George W. Jones at Linotype & Machinery Ltd. which gained a host of adherent practitioners

Undoubtedly the deepest upheavals in typesetting over recent years have been occasioned by the computer and its peripherals, notably the video terminal. They have revolutionised the capture, input, correction, composition, and make-up of text. The sheer ferocity and intensity of the incursion can be gauged by the density of chronological entries which increases markedly for the two decades leading up to 1986. Desktop publishing systems, a marriage between personal computer and electronic printer, began to emerge in 1985 and appear poised to bring about further changes in the methods of type composition.

To facilitate ease of access to the information gathered, the entries in the chronology have been divided into fifteen different categories. Each category is identified in the margin by a two- or three-letter mnemonic. As a consequence, the reader will be able to spot readily the subject of immediate interest. The categories are as follows.

LIN   Linecasting (i.e. Linotype, Intertype, Ludlow, and Teletypesetter developements).

MON Monotype Composition.

MC   Mechanical Composition (i.e. hot-metal machines and systems not covered by the two previous categories).

TF   Typefounding.

TYP Type Design and Typography.

J&P Journals and Publications.

PTS Phototypesetting (i.e. typographic exposure units and electronic printers).

SO   Strike-On Compostion, including metal type conversion systems and reproduction proofing machines (e.g. Orotype).

TO   Trade Organisations and Services (i.e. trades unions, specialist libraries and schools, exhibitions, and general events).

KEY Input Keyboards.

VDU Video Display Units (i.e. stand-alone models).

CAT Computer-Aided Typesetting (i.e. batch composition systems without video terminals).

OCR Optical Character Recognition.

FES Front-End Compostion Systems (i.e. computer-based systems with clustered video terminals).

GRA Monochrome Digital Graphics Systems

One other matter of presentation: the accents in foreign names have been deliberately omitted.

It is hoped that readers will enjoy the chronology and I apologise in advance for any pet events that have been omitted, but the word 'concise' in the title was intended to have some significance. The prime purpose has been to celebrate the centenary of the Linotype machine.

L. W. Wallis
Maulden, Bedfordshire

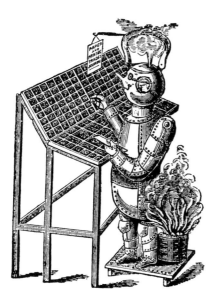

The New Steam Compositor

1886

LIN Ottmar Mergenthaler designed the Blower Linotype. It was installed at the *New York Tribune* during July. Previous attempts by Mergenthaler to mechanise typesetting had encountered mixed fortunes, as evidenced by a Rotary Matrix Machine (1883), the First Band Machine (1883), and the Second Band Machine (1884). Only 212 of the Blower Linotype machines were built before technical improvements occasioned obsolescence.

LIN Mergenthaler Printing Company founded to support the Blower Linotype machine. It superseded the National Typographic Company.

MC Alexander Lagerman developed the Typotheter, a device that clamped on to a composing frame and was intended to aid the hand assembly of metal types. In practice the compositor simply dropped types picked out of a case into a funnel of the Typotheter and mechanical feelers arranged them to the correct aspect in line form ready for manual justification.

TF United States Type Founders' Association met at Niagara to consider the systematic and regularised measurement of metal type bodies. It was decided to adopt the pica of the Mackellar, Smiths & Jordan typefoundry as the standard which when divided into twelve equal parts yielded a point of 0.013837 inch.

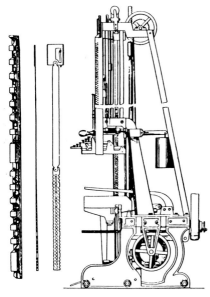

Second Band Machine

1887

J&P First book composed on the Linotype machine, namely *The Tribune Book of Open Air Sports* published in New York. Conscious of the uniqueness of the occasion, the book bore an inscription stating that the printing had been accomplished 'without type being the first product in book form of the Mergenthaler machine which wholly supersedes the use of movable type'.

MON Patents granted to Tolbert Lanston for a system composing single types mechanically. It consisted of a keyboard for producing a perforated record of a job in a paper spool which controlled an associate stamping machine for fashioning types from cold strips of metal. The invention prompted formation of the Lanston Monotype Company.

MC Manufacture of the first Paige Compositor machine was completed, a gigantic contrivance that set, justified, and distributed pre-cast metal types. Inventor was J. W. Paige who originally set out to mechanise type composition in 1873 and modified those ideas radically in 1877. Stretching to 9 feet in length, the eventual machine contained 18,000 parts and weighed 50,000 pounds. Some $2,000,000 were invested in the project emanating from, among others, Samuel L. Clemens (Mark Twain). In 1894 a second and last machine was built and installed at the *Chicago Herald*.

SO George Allen issued proposals for a typesetter/printer. The machine was keyboard operated and assembled type bars into lines for impression as a repro proof on to paper. It was a conceptual forerunner of the Typary (see 1925) and Orotype (see 1937) machines.

TO George W. Jones and associates founded the British Typographia for the technical and artistic advancement of printing. It did much to establish formalised training in the industry.

Portrait of Tolbert Lanston

Arms of British Typographia

1888

LIN Ottmar Mergenthaler sold his interest in the Mergenthaler Printing Company of Baltimore which supported the Blower Linotype development and removed to Brooklyn to set up Ottmar Mergenthaler & Co.

TF Hans Barth, of the Cincinnati Type Foundry, designed a typecasting machine which delivered finished 'stamps' ready for packaging into printers' founts. It perpetuated the traditions of high-grade typefounding. Extensive use was made of the machine by the American Type Founders Co. (see 1892).

TF   R. D. DeLittle, a manufacturer of wood letter for poster composition, established in York. The firm is currently the only surviving producer of wood letter in the United Kingdom.

TYP   On 15 November William Morris attended a lecture on letterpress printing given by Emery Walker to the Arts and Crafts Exhibition Society. It galvanised Morris to engage in printing by founding the Kelmscott Press which did much to stimulate a revival in British printing and typographic design (see 1896, 1930 and 1933).

J&P   *The British Printer* magazine first published by Raithby, Lawrence & Co. of Leicester where George W. Jones was Works Manager. Robert Hilton edited the journal.

William Morris

1889

LIN   Linotype Company Ltd. founded in Manchester. It was a manufacturing organisation.

TO   Typefounders' Society, a trade union, established in London with about 200 members. In 1937 the name changed to the Monotype Casters' and Typefounders' Society.

TYP   Stanley Morison born on 6 May. He was destined to become the most dominant influence on type design during the twentieth century.

TO   Ecole Estienne established in Paris for the training of typographers, printers, lithographers, process technicians, bookbinders, and others in the industry.

1890

LIN   Square-Base Model 1 Linotype was introduced: the first machine to have a 90-character power-driven keyboard. This machine marked the beginning of the 'modern' linecaster.

LIN   Mergenthaler Linotype Co. established in Brooklyn.

LIN   First Linotype Square-Base Model 1 installed at the *Standard-Union* in Brooklyn.

LIN   First American-built Square-Based Linotype Model 1 installed in Britain at the *Leeds Mercury*.

MON   Introduction of the Monotype Triangle machine developed by Tolbert Lanston. It abandoned previous notions of stamping letter shapes into cold metal and graduated to casting techniques. In 1891 a mutation of the idea was called the Hot-Metal Machine. At the World Fair in Chicago of 1893, the results of these two endeavours were exhibited in a mammoth, complex, and costly contrivance.

MC   John R. Rogers completed development of the Typograph linecasting machine. It was a keyboard-operated device with matrices suspended on wires. In response to a key depression the matrices slid down the wires to an assembly point. Rotary spacers were used for justification. After casting the line of type, the operator tilted back the frame of wires causing the matrices to return to their storage positions.

MC   R. H. St. John invented the Typobar composing machine which assembled intaglio matrices from a keyboard in a manner redolent of a linecaster. On completing the assembly of a line, a bar of soft cold metal was impressed into the matrices, thereby creating a slug of type.

Typograph machine

1891

LIN   Ottmar Mergenthaler secured an injunction against John R. Rogers preventing manufacture of the Typograph machine in the USA. He had prior claim to the principle of casting a type slug from individual matrices. Another source of interest was the justification of lines by opposing-wedge spacers embodied in the Typograph ensuant on a

patent acquired from J. W. Schuckers who had just beaten
Mergenthaler to protecting the idea in 1885. As a consequence,
Mergenthaler bought the Typograph patents, factory, and machines
for $416,000. Manufacture of the Typograph continued in Canada
and Germany.

TYP   William Morris founded the Kelmscott Press at Hammersmith in
London. It issued a number of impressive and decorative volumes,
notably *The Works of Geoffrey Chaucer* in 1896.

TYP   Francis Meynell born on 12 May (see 1975).

TO   St. Bride Printing Library established in London.

1892

LIN   First British-built Square-Base Linotype Model 1 installed at the
Newcastle Evening Chronicle.

LIN   First London newspaper, *The Globe*, adopted the Linotype machine,
followed soon afterwards by the *Financial News.*

LIN   Linotype Model 1 was re-fashioned to exclude the massive square base
featured in the machine two years previously. It contained a number of
other mechanical refinements and proved to be a commercially
popular unit. Manufacture of the Star-Base Linotype Model 1 did not
occur in Britain until 1895.

MC   Monoline composition and slug casting machine invented by Wilbur
Scudder. It was a practical machine, but encountered patent litigation
from Linotype which restricted manufacture to outside the USA.
Matrix bars were deployed each containing a dozen characters of
common width with eight thicknesses featuring in the machine.
Notches on the back of the matrix bars corresponded to the characters
and allowed registration with an alignment bar. Keyboard assembly
from a storage magazine was practised. Line justification relied on
wedges and automatic distribution completed the cycle.

TF   American Type Founders Company was constituted from twenty-
three existing firms.

TF   Rudhard Foundry at Offenbach taken over by Karl Klingspor. Its
design policy was vigorous, imaginative, and involved several notable
artists, such as Rudolf Koch, Peter Behrens, and Walter Tiemann.
Results of the work were to be seen in a repertory of distinguished
display type families.

TYP   Jan van Krimpen born on 12 January. He was to design a number of
distinguished typefaces for Enschede en Zonen and the Monotype
Corporation Ltd. as instanced by Lutetia (1925), Romanee (1928),
Romulus (1931), and Spectrum (1952).

TF   Talbot Baines Reed, the typefounder and author, died on 28
November. He joined the family typefoundry of Sir Charles Reed &
Sons Ltd. in 1879 and published his authoritative volume *The History
of Old English Letter Foundries* in 1887. Other distinctions include
the first secretaryship of the Bibliographical Society in 1892 and the
authorship of many popular boys' books.

TYP   Giovanni Mardersteig born on 27 December (see 1923).

TO   Eastman Kodak Company established after trading under several
previous names from 1881.

1893

LIN   First weekly newspaper in Britain installed a Linotype machine,
namely the *Derbyshire Times.*

LIN   Linotype Company established training schools in London and
Manchester. It was, in part, an action taken defensively against
unreasonable demands by the Typographical Association for
uneconomic working conditions which threatened to impede the
spread of the Linotype machine.

MON   Four-Tower Monotype machine developed by Tolbert Lanston and

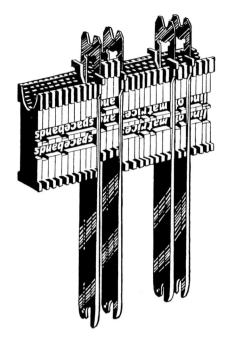

Linotype matrices and spacebands

ABCDEFGH
abcdefghijklmn

Lutetia

John Bancroft, the last of the experimental models before the inventors hit upon the idea that was to become the successful and durable Monotype system.

TF   American Type Founders Company took over its biggest single customer, the Thorne Typesetting Machine Company which was merged with the Cox Typesetting Machine Company (controlled by the Barnhart Bros. & Spindler typefoundry) to form the Unitype Company. All three machines assembled cold founders' metal types (see 1898).

J&P   Horace Hart issued the first edition of *Rules for Compositors and Readers at the University Press, Oxford.* Originally planned as an internal document, the fifteenth edition went on general sale in 1904 and became a standard work of reference on house style.

PTS   Arthur Ferguson was granted a patent for a system that farsightedly envisaged the photographic composition of type.

1894

LIN   *De Neederlandsche Financier* received the first Linotype machine in continental Europe. It was manufactured in Britain.

TF   Inland Type Foundry introduced the standard lining system for founders' type. It was adopted widely in the industry by 1900.

MC   Frank A. Johnson worked on a single type casting and composing system called the Tachytype. Tape control featured in the concept. British rights to the scheme were purchased by Linotype to test validity of the technical approach, but nothing emerged from the interest.

TYP   Maximilien Vox, the distinguished French typographer, born on 16 December (see 1974).

PTS   One of the earliest patents for a phototypesetting system was granted to E. Porzsolt. Central to the proposal was the use of keybars bearing characters, the exposed images being formed by reflected light.

1895

LIN   First British-built star-shaped base Linotype Model 1 delivered to the *Wakefield Chronicle.*

MC   Announcement was made of a Pulsometer typesetting machine invented by S. H and P. E. Hodgkin. It was a system for assembling pre-cast metal types stored in magazines with a horizontal aspect, instead of the more usual vertical. Depressions on a keyboard caused the types to be pushed forward into a converging channel. Justification of lines was by hand, while a second machine had to be installed for distribution. In 1904 the Pulsometer Engineering Company of Reading brought the machine to market without effect.

TF   Stempel typefoundry established at Frankfurt-am-Main by David Stempel. The Linotype Group of Companies had a significant shareholding in the concern for many years and eventually acquired the typefoundry wholly in 1985.

J&P   First type specimen book issued by the American Type Founders Company (see 1892).

PTS   William Friese-Greene gained a patent for a phototypesetting system. It stored complete alphabets vertically down keybars which were arranged side by side. In response to the activation of keybuttons, the keybars dropped by gravity to a stop level where a complete line of text was assembled against a slot. Light was shone on to the white characters mounted on black backgrounds to produce a photographic positive by reflection.

1896

LIN   Mergenthaler Setzmaschinenfabrik GmbH founded in Berlin.

LIN   Linotype Users Association established.

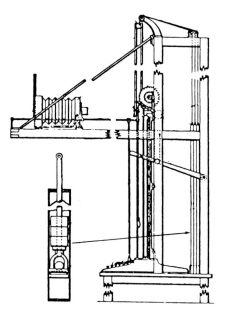

Friese-Greene patent drawing

TYP   Cheltenham typeface designed by Bertram Goodhue for the American printer H. Ingalls Kimball of the Cheltenham Press. Commercial development of the design occurred at American Type Founders under the direction of M. F. Benton between 1904 and 1911. Though devoid of grace, Cheltenham became an exceedingly popular design and prompted many imitations, as exemplified by Gloucester (Monotype) and Winchester (Stephenson Blake).

TYP   William Morris, the creative spirit behind the Kelmscott Press, died on 3 October.

abcdefghijklmnopqrstuv
ABCDEFGHIJKLMNOPQ
1234567890 .,;:"«»&!?

Cheltenham

1897

LIN   Longest slug obtainable from a Linotype machine was extended to 42 picas. Earlier the limitation had been 30 picas.

LIN   Linotype Company established a factory at Altrincham in the north-west of England. Previously the works had been sited in Manchester (see 1889).

MON   Original concept of Tolbert Lanston to build a die-stamping machine was transmogrified by John Sellers Bancroft into a casting apparatus, but still controlled from a perforated paper job record. One effect of the switch in development was to drop the number of available typographic characters from 225 to 132, thereby earning the description Limited Fount Machine. Also a justification wedge was perfected for expanding word spaces only, instead of adding space to every character in a line. The modern Monotype system dates from this time.

MON   Lanston Monotype Corporation Ltd. founded in Britain.

Portrait of John Bancroft

1898

LIN   Two-letter or duplex matrices were made available to Linotype machines. Previous matrices had been restricted to the image of a single character.

LIN   Universal Adjustable Mould was introduced to the Linotype machine. It enabled variable line lengths and type body sizes within the specifications of the equipment to be obtained by inserting the appropriate liners. Previously moulds had been fixed to a given point size and to a given measure.

MON   First of the Limited Fount Monotype Machines were installed at Gibson Brothers in Washington D.C. and at Wyman & Sons Ltd. in London.

MC   Simplex One-Man Typesetter or Unitype composing machine came on the market. It was based on the Thorne device of 1880 which served commercially at the *Manchester Guardian, Bradford Observer,* and other enterprises. The Simplex or Unitype system embodied several improvements over the earlier device. Assembly and distribution of pre-cast metal types was performed, but line justification had to be done by hand.

TF   British typefoundries agree to adopt the American point system.

TF   H. Berthold AG released the enduring Akzidenz Grotesk sanserif typeface.

abcdefghijklmnopqrstuv
ABCDEFGHIJKLMNOP
1234567890 .,;:''«»&!?

Akzidenz Grotesk

1899

MON   John Sellers Bancroft re-engineered the Monotype caster and restored the character complement to that originally intended of 225.

MON   Lanston Monotype Corporation Ltd. established a factory at Salfords near Redhill in Surrey.

TF   Caxton Type Foundry, started at Market Harborough by Walter Haddon, was the first British foundry to adopt the point system.

LIN   Ottmar Mergenthaler, the inventor of the Linotype machine, died on 28 October in Baltimore, USA.

TYP   At the London Central School of Arts and Crafts, Edward Johnston started classes in calligraphy and illumination. As the foremost scribe of the period, a number of exceptional students emerged from his instruction, as instanced by Eric Gill and Graily Hewitt. Much of the interest stimulated by Edward Johnston in letter forms spilt over into type design and with beneficial effect. In 1901 Johnston initiated similar classes at the Royal College of Art.

PTS   First proposals for a phototypesetting system forming images by transmitted light emerged from Richards. Characters were mounted around a sector which oscillated in response to keyboard operations.

1900

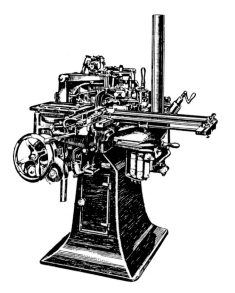

LIN   D. Stempel AG and Mergenthaler Setzmaschinenfabrik GmbH signed a contract whereby the former would make Linotype matrices.

MON   Initial installation of the Monotype system re-designed by Bancroft in 1899 commissioned at Cassell & Co. Ltd. of London.

TYP   T. J. Cobden-Sanderson and Emery Walker set up the Doves Press at Hammersmith. Its special typeface, a close derivative of the Nicholas Jenson fifteenth-century model, was cut by Edward Prince.

TYP   Beatrice Warde born on 20 September. She was appointed Publicity Manager for The Monotype Corporation Ltd. in the middle 1920s, among the responsibilities being editorship of *The Monotype Recorder.* Her writings on matters typographic were prodigious, the most notable being original research into the Garamond types published in *The Fleuron* (see 1923) under the pseudonym of Paul Beaujon. Perhaps her most popular piece of work was the inscription beginning 'This is a printing office' prepared in 1932 and translated into countless languages. Her essays have been collected and published in book form as *The Crystal Goblet.*

TYP   Birth of Imre Reiner, the Hungarian illustrator and graphic designer. His typefaces are numerous and include: Corvinus (Bauer 1929), Meridian (Klingspor 1930), Matura (Monotype 1938), Pepita (Monotype 1959), Stradivarius (Bauer 1945), and Mercurius (Monotype 1957). He settled in Switzerland during 1931.

Monotype Composition Caster

1901

LIN   Linotype Junior introduced, a derivative of the Typograph machine (see 1890). Development was by the Mergenthaler Linotype Co. Apparently the machine was intended to compete with the Simplex One-Man Typesetter (see 1898) which it did successfully and forced the latter model off the market. Nickname for the Linotype Junior was the Birdcage because of the profusion of wires characterising its construction. Market span was quite short.

LIN   Individual electric motors for Linotype machines were devised which assured constant speed and smooth operation. Hitherto the machines had been driven from collective shafting.

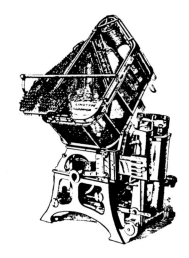

MC   Automatic Type Machine, also known as the Compositype, was announced. It was a sorts caster developed for the United Printing Machinery Company in Baltimore by F. H. Brown, J. E. Hanrahan, and G. A. Boyden (see 1908). Despite optimistic expectations of the backers, the machine was not a great success.

LIN   Donald Murray, an Australian journalist, proposed the setting of type by telegraphy (see 1926 and 1928).

Linotype Junior

1902

LIN   Specification of the Linotype machine was extended to encompass a wheel with four moulds, as opposed to earlier equipment embodying two moulds only. Accordingly the production of type was streamlined with easier access to a variety of measures and body sizes.

MC   Patents were granted to H. J. S. Gilbert-Stringer for the Stringertype machine. Its overall appearance resembled that of a linecaster, but the output consisted of newly-cast, composed, and justified single metal types. Direct keyboarding was an operational characteristic, as was the circulation of matrices through the machine. In general shape, the matrices looked like those from a linecaster, except that the image was depressed into the side or flat of the matrix and not into the edge. Assembly and distribution of the matrices was conducted in the manner of a linecaster. Having assembled a text line, the matrices were separated and presented singly to the casting apparatus. Notches in the matrices served as guides for automatically adjusting the mould to the character widths. As late as 1936, the Stringertype was demonstrated in London at the 9th International Printing Exhibition, though the name was changed to Supertype. It was promoted as 'the only "one-man" single type composing and casting machine extant'.

J&P   *The Monotype Recorder* first published.

TYP   Jan Tschichold born 2 April in Leipzig (see 1974).

J&P   John S. Thompson had published a textbook entitled *The Mechanism of the Linotype*. It was a seminal work of standard reference published by the Inland Printer Company. Thirteen editions of the book were to appear over the ensuing years.

PTS   Rene A. Higonnet born on 5 April; a man who in partnership with Louis Moyroud invented a vanguard and successful electronic phototypesetting system which helped to transform typographic composing practices.

1903

LIN   Linotype Model 2 was launched in the USA, the first machine to incorporate two magazines of matrices. Furthermore the mechanism enabled the mixing of matrices from the two magazines in a single line of type and undertook their respective distribution automatically.

LIN   Linotype Model 3 was released in the USA. It used a wider matrix magazine than erstwhile devices: a characteristic increasing the largest type size obtainable from 11 to 12 point. Not surprisingly, the nickname Pica Machine was invoked.

LIN   Linotype & Machinery Ltd. formed in Britain by the amalgamation of the Linotype Company (see 1889) and the Machinery Trust Ltd.

SO   Lithotype machines patented by Walter S. Timmis. Two units consituted the system, a punched paper tape keyboard and a printing unit reproducing the text on lithographic transfer paper as dictated by the perforated record of the job.

TYP   Konrad F. Bauer born on 9 December. Designer of several typefaces in association with Walter Baum for the Bauer typefoundry, including: Horizon (1925), Alpha (1954), Beta (1954), Fortune (1955), Folio (1957), and Impressum (1962).

J&P   *Correct Keyboard Fingering: A System of Fingering the Linotype Keyboard for the Acquisition of Speed of Operating*, a 16-page pamphlet written by John S. Thompson, was published.

1904

MON   Lanston Monotype Corporation Ltd. first took offices at 43 Fetter Lane off Fleet Street in London: the site was destined to develop strong associations with fine printing.

TO   First of the International Printing Machinery and Allied Trades Exhibitions (IPEX) held.

TF   Sir H. Stephenson, of the typefoundry Stephenson, Blake & Co., died on 24 August.

J&P   The book a *History of Composing Machines: A Complete Record of the Art of Composing Type by Machinery*, from the pen of John S. Thompson, was published.

abcdefghijklmnopqrstu
ABCDEFGHIJKLMNO
1234567890 .,;:'"«»&!?
Folio

abcdefghijklmnopqr
ABCDEFGHIJKLMN
XYZ 1234567890 .,;:'"
Impressum

1905

LIN   Recessed mould was released for the Linotype machine. It reduced the weight of a slug and improved the quality of the printing surface, especially in larger point sizes. In appearance the slug was flat along one side and ribbed on the other. Only solid slugs were produced on forerunning machines.

MON   Display type attachment and casting speed regulator embraced by the Monotype caster. Type sizes up to 24 point could be produced, though only composed mechanically up to 12 point.

TF   Stephenson, Blake & Co. bought Sir Charles Reed & Sons Ltd. (the Fann Street Foundry) to enhance greatly the typographic resources and stocks of the Sheffield typefoundry.

TF   John Southward wrote in *Modern Printing* that conversion to the point system by the typefounding industry had just about been completed.

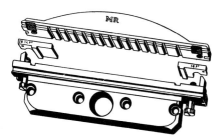

Recessed Linotype mould

Recessed Linotype slug

Ha!

1906

LIN   Linotype Model 2 built in Britain. It accommodated a single magazine which could be changed from the front of the machine. Linotype Model 5 was the equivalent American version (q.v.).

LIN   Linotype Model 4 emerged in the USA. It was a mixing machine with two magazines. The designation in the United Kingdom was the Linotype Model 3.

LIN   Linotype Model 5 announced in the USA. It had a single magazine which was replaced from the front, as opposed to the back as previously. Machines could now be sited back to back or placed near to a wall. In the United Kingdom, the unit was known as the Model 2, the first delivery taking place in 1907.

LIN   Automatic quadding of the last lines of paragraphs introduced on Linotype machines. That is quadding to the left only was implemented (see 1932).

LIN   Standard 90-channel Linotype magazine heralded carrying 22 matrices per channel for type sizes up to 18 point (condensed faces only).

TF   Universal Type Caster developed by Philip Nuernberger and George Rettig. It used a harder alloy than other contemporaneous sorts casters. Both the inventors were experienced in the traditional procedures of typefounding (see 1918).

LIN   Ludlow Typograph Company established to develop a composing machine based on the principle of manipulating type bars under keyboard control. Five machines were built, but abandonment of the scheme ensued because of lack of commercial potential. Originator of the machine was Washington I. Ludlow who took the prototype to William Reade for refinement and finish. It was Reade who developed the concept for the more durable Ludlow system (see 1909).

J&P   The book *Writing and Illuminating and Lettering* by Edward Johnston published.

1907

LIN   Linotype Model 3 built in Britain, the first double-distributor machine to emerge from the Altrincham factory. It permitted mixing from the two magazines accommodated. The equivalent American version was the Linotype Model 4 (see 1906).

LIN   Sorts stacker developed for Linotype machine. It arranged pi-matrices in an orderly fashion ensuant on distribution. Earlier the sorts were channelled into a box as jumble which could lead to damage of the matrices.

MON   Monotype Model D Keyboard launched. It incorporated the universal typewriter layout of buttons with the attendant advantages of touch

Monotype D Keyboard

operation and internally the number of air valves shrunk from 225 to 33. Previously the Model C Keyboard had a button layout that matched the matrix case arrangement on the caster.

TC   Thompson Type Machine Co. formed in Chicago to market the Thompson Typecaster (see 1908).

TF   Stephenson, Blake & Co. Ltd., the typefoundry, diversified into the manufacture of wooden composing cabinets and equipment.

Monotype DD (Duplex) Keyboard

1908

MON   Launch of the Monotype Duplex Keyboard with two paper towers and two unit-registering mechanisms, but with one set of keybanks.

MON   Low-quad moulds incepted for Monotype machines.

MC   Typograph machines re-introduced in the United Kingdom following the patent dispute of 1891 (q.v.).

TF   American Type Founders Co. established a typographical library under the custodianship of Henry Lewis Bullen. It constituted an outstanding collection of historical and technical literature of printing. Columbia University became heir to the library.

TF   John S. Thompson developed a sorts caster bearing his name. Printers used the machine to replenish stocks of type for handsetting from case. The Thompson Type Caster was a sound machine that outlasted many rivals (see 1929). It used Linotype matrices and later Compositype and Monotype matrices.

MC   Thompson Type Machine Company purchased the assets of the National Compositype Company of Baltimore and manufacture of the Compositype machine ceased.

1909

LIN   Universal Ejector Blade introduced to Linotype machines. Originally the blade used for ejecting slugs from the mould was of monolithic construction. As a consequence, a change of measure necessitated the fitting of a complementary ejector blade. The universal blade was made in sections allowing different combinations to be activated for various measures, thereby steamlining machine changeovers.

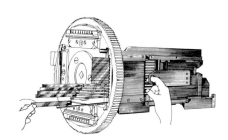

Universal Ejector Blade

LIN   Water-cooled mould wheel added to Linotype machines. Formerly the moulds were not cooled artificially. The development improved the quality of slugs.

LIN   Universal Knife Block was designed for Linotype machines. It enabled the parallel knives for trimming slugs to be adjusted readily over the range from 5 to 36 points.

LIN   Display mould and matrices developed for Linotype machine. Using the recessed structure, a display mould could produce type sizes up to 36 point.

MON   Composition in 14 point type enabled on Monotype caster.

LIN   William Reade was well advanced in development of the Ludlow machine for casting slugs from hand assembled matrices (see 1911).

1910

LIN   Linotype Model 4 introduced by Linotype & Machinery Ltd. (see 1911).

MON   Reverse delivery mechanism developed for Monotype caster permitting the composition of languages read from right-to-left (e.g. Arabic and Hebrew).

MC   Victorline composing and slugcasting machine was displayed for the first time at a British printing exhibition. Production of the unit was carried out in Berlin by the General Composing Company, an enterprise that had manufactured the German version of the Monoline (see 1892) for many years. Design of the Victorline was the work of Heinrich Degenner, though the machine was virtually identical to the two-letter single-magazine Linotype. It incorporated a few improvements, such as a water-cooled mould and a quick-change magazine. Very soon the German arm of the Linotype Group of Companies acquired the assets and patents of the Victorline.

TF   Thompson Typecaster was demonstrated in London by the General Electric Company, the British agents for the Victorline (q.v.) slugcasting and composing machine manufactured in Berlin by the General Composing Company.

TF   John C. Grant and Lucien A. Legros designed and patented a punchcutting machine (see 1916).

1911

LIN   Linotype Model 8 was announced in the USA. It accommodated three magazines of matrices, the first machine to do so. Each magazine could be readily brought into operation. Included in the development was an automatic fount distinguisher which prevented matrices entering the wrong magazine during distribution. The British equivalent was the Linotype Model 4.

LIN   Linotype Model 9 released in the USA. It was the first machine to embody four magazines. Matrices from them could be intermixed in a single line of type by bringing the successive magazines conveniently into the active position. Afterwards the matrices were returned automatically to their respective storage channels. The British company used the same machine designation.

LIN   First Linotype machine used for composition of the Arabic script, though the character complement was cramped.

LIN   International Typesetting Machine Company formed to manufacture three new composing devices: the Amalgatype, the Monoline, and a unit that eventually became known as the Intertype. Research into the principal defects and most troublesome features of extant linecasters was to provide the basis for the latter ameliorative development. Nine patent applications for improvements in linecasting machines ensued.

MON   Problem of dealing with kerned characters solved for Monotype machines. It was to give the company a competitive edge over linecasting equipment, especially in the rendering of elegant italics and literature was consistently produced to support the argument.

LIN   In January the Ludlow Typograph Company publicly demonstrated a machine casting lines of type from hand-assembled matrices. Twenty of the Ludlow units were built during the year.

1912

LIN   Prototype of Intertype machine demonstrated publicly in October, the procreative patents of Mergenthaler having expired.

MON   Monotype caster endowed with the capability of composing type sizes up to and including 18 point.

MC   Hans Peterson developed the Linograph. In essence the device was a Linotype in small scale which stood about 5.5 feet tall. It featured vertical magazines, incorporated direct transfer of a line of matrices from the casting position to the distributor bar, and delivered slugs with low quadding of appeal to pressmen. Matrices employed were peculiar to the Linograph and represented miniaturised Linotype characters which ran in short magazines.

TYP   Imprint, the first typeface designed specifically for mechanical composition, was cut by the Lanston Monotype Corporation. Plans for the type style were determined by Gerard Meynell and J. H. Mason, the progenitors and editors with F. Ernest Jackson and Edward Johnston of a typographical magazine called *The Imprint*. Nine issues of the journal, set in the bespoke typeface, appeared during 1913. More than 8,000 sets of hot-metal matrices of the Imprint design had been sold by the 1980s.

Early Ludlow typesetting system

abcdefghijklmnopqrstuv
ABCDEFGHIJKLMN
XYZ 1234567890 12345

Imprint

OCR   Early patents for an optical character recognition device filed by Hiram Goldberg.

1913

LIN   Linotype Model 65 built in Britain, the machine accommodated four magazines and incorporated a double disributor. Mixing could be conducted only between the upper pair or lower pair of magazines.

LIN   First production model of an Intertype machine was installed at the *Journal of Commerce* in New York.

MON   Monotype Type and Rule Caster announced. It allowed printers to stock hand composing rooms with founts of type, quads, leads, clumps, and rules. To enhance the new machine as an investment proposition, a Display Matrix Lending Library was established in London by the Lanston Monotype Corporation.

LIN   *Evening Post* of Chicago installed the first Ludlow machine.

LIN   Sloping matrices developed for the Ludlow machine to accommodate and to cast fluent italic type designs.

SO   James B. Hammond, inventor of a typewriter bearing his name, died. His patents were bequeathed to the Metropolitan Museum of New York and later bought by the Frederick Hepburn Company. The reincarnated machine was called the Varityper and eventually passed by commercial acquisition to Ralph C. Coxhead in 1933.

TYP   Plantin Series 110 typeface released for composition on the Monotype system. It was prompted by F. H. Pierpont and has enjoyed enduring popularity. More than 10,500 sets of hot-metal matrices of the design had been sold by the 1980s.

TYP   Edward Johnston, commissioned by Frank Pick, designed a sanserif alphabet for the London Underground Railway.

MON   Tolbert Lanston, the inventor of the Monotype system, died in Washington on 18 February.

1914

LIN   Linotype Model 14 evolved, the initial machine to incorporate an auxiliary or side magazine containing 28 channels, as distinct from main magazines with 90 channels. Essentially the development extended the typographical mixing possibilities of linecasting. (*NB*. In general terms a channel equated to a typographic character).

MON   Ceiling composition type size on Monotype caster increased to 24 point.

MON   Monotype Users' Association founded.

TYP   Theodore Low De Vinne died on 16 February. The renowned American printer contributed handsomely to trade literature, notably with four volumes on *The Practice of Typography* which began to surface in 1900. As a result of collaboration with Linn Boyd Benton came the Century typeface in 1894 cut for the magazine of the same name.

1915

LIN   Electrically-heated metal pot perfected for the Linotype machine. Formerly the task of maintaining the type alloy in a molten condition was accomplished by gas heating with the associated disadvantages of open flames and noxious fumes. Electricity afforded better control over the casting process.

MON   Lead-and-rule attachment uncovered for the Monotype composition caster. It was novel for the incremental fused casting of type metal in unlimited lengths.

PTS   Alfred E. Bawtree secured a patent for a photo-lettering display machine. It stored typographic founts on a photo-matrix disc which was manually rotated to bring the required characters to a common

Frank Pierpont

abcdefghijklmnopqrstuvw
ABCDEFGHIJKLMNOP
1234567890 1234567890 .,

Plantin 110

abcdefghijklmnopqrstuvw
ABCDEFGHIJKLMNOP
1234567890 .,;:"«»&!?

Century

exposure position. Imaging was prompted by a handle to the right of the device, the movement of which determined escapement as well.

PTS   Two German engineers, Siemens and Halske, patented proposals for a phototypesetting machine which exposed typographic images on to a continuously moving photosensitive material by means of a short duration electric spark. Implicit in the design was that the width of a character had to be escaped by the sensitive plane before exposure occurred. It was a farsighted notion.

1916

LIN   International Typesetting Machine Company entered receivership. Its stock was bought for $1,650,000 to emerge as the newly formed Intertype Corporation.

TYP   Caslon Series 128 typeface launched by the Lanston Monotype Corporation.

TYP   Pelican Press founded under the stewardship of Francis Meynell. It set out to produce 'the finest printing for commerce' and did a great deal to establish the respectability of mechanical composition. Stanley Morison succeeded Francis Meynell as supervisor in 1919. The press issued, in 1921, a most distinguished promotional book entitled simply *Typography*.

J&P   The book *Typographical Printing Surfaces: the Technology and Mechanism of their Production*, by Lucien A. Legros and John C. Grant, was published. It became a standard treatise on typefounding and provided an early analysis and insight into mechanical composing techniques.

abcdefghijklmnopqrstuvwx
ABCDEFGHIJKLMNO
1234567890 .,;:"«»&!?

Caslon

1917

LIN   Distributor mechanism improved on the Linotype machine by the introduction of two-pitch screws which quickened the process and maintained accuracy. Matrices were separated more widely along the distributor bar lessening the incidence of jams.

LIN   Agreement reached between the Ludlow Typograph Co. and the Mergenthaler Linotype Co. whereby the latter became sales agent for Ludlow machines. The association was cancelled in January 1919.

LIN   Elrod Strip Material Caster invented by Benjamin S. Elrod, a remarkable personality who had established the first Linotype tradesetting house west of the Mississippi River.

PTS   Isaac S. Bunnell, a printer from New Jersey, patented a display photolettering machine.

1918

LIN   Linotype Model 20 surfaced, the first display machine. It accommodated a single magazine of 72 channels, instead of the usual 90. Owing to the smaller overall number, the widths of the individual channels could be widened to run bigger faces. Type sizes up to 30 point could be assembled routinely from the keyboard. Furthermore a split magazine was developed to facilitate machine changeovers. In essence the normal magazine was divided transversely: the top half nearest the distributor mechanism remained on the machine leaving the bottom half (split) to be comfortably removed for typeface changes.

LIN   Intertype Corporation received an order for 31 linecasters from the *New York Times*. It helped to establish the fledgeling machinery supplier.

LIN   First Ludlow machine installed for general commercial printing applications at Saul Brothers in Chicago.

TF   Thompson Type Machine Company secured rights to the Universal typecasting machine.

TO British government requests 25,000 tons of metal from the printing industry in the form of types and duplicate plates for the manufacture of armaments.

TYP Hermann Zapf born on 8 November. His outstanding career was to involve a period as type director for the D. Stempel AG typefoundry and as a design consultant for the Mergenthaler Linotype Company and for Hallmark International. His type design credits encompass Palatino (1950), Melior (1952), Aldus (1954), Optima (1958), Orion (1974), Comenius (1976), Zapf International (1977), Zapf Chancery (1979), and Zapf Renaissance (1986).

1919

LIN M. H. Whittaker & Son Ltd. established in Leeds. The founder had worked previously with Ottmar Mergenthaler on the original Blower machine and subsequently worked for the Linotype Company Ltd. His family business was to serve as representative for the Intertype machine in the north of England and much later (1970) as national agent for Compugraphic phototypesetters. It undertook some novel technical development as well, evidenced by the SAM (Sets All Matrtices) linecaster (see 1966).

1920

LIN Ludlow Typograph Company assumed responsibility for the manufacture and sale of the Elrod lead and rule caster.

PTS Arthur Dutton experimented with a Photoline machine for the photographic composition of type. The project was not a success, but the inventor undaunted was reported in *The Penrose Annual* of 1935 to be returning to the subject with a fresh device known as the Flickertype or Flickerletter. More than one contemporary writer compared the invention of the 1920s to the Typograph machine.

1921

LIN Linotype Models 21 and 22 introduced in the USA. They superseded the Model 20 of 1918.

LIN Intertype Ltd. formed in the United Kingdom. Single distributor Model C machine was marketed initially.

MON Composition system for large sizes between 14 and 24 point inclusive developed for the Monotype Caster.

MC Linograph Model 3 released with three vertical magazines of matrices (see 1912).

TYP George W. Jones appointed 'printing adviser' to Linotype & Machinery Ltd. in September. He ran a highly-regarded printing business At the Sign of the Dolphin in London and was responsible for the development of several classic typefaces for the Linotype machine, such as Granjon (1924), Georgian (1925), Estienne (1926), and Venezia (1928).

PTS Patent applications for a 'photographic composing' machine were made in the names of Edgar Kenneth Hunter and Robert Carl August on Christmas Eve and during the early months of 1922. In principle the August-Hunter invention was a direct-entry device encompassing a keyboard and an exposure unit. Punched paper tape served as line buffer store between the input and output processes. Hard copy print-out of keystrokes occurred on a strip of paper. Optical storage of character widths was another feature. Funding for the research was through the AH Developments Syndicate Ltd. Press reports of the machine appeared regularly over the two decades of the 1920s and 1930s. As far as can be ascertained, a machine was never installed commercially.

PTS John Robertson, Thomas Brown, and Andrew Orrell proposed the

abcdefghijklmnopqrst
ABCDEFGHIJKLMNOP
1234567890 1234567890

Optima

abcdefghijklmnopqrstu
ABCDEFGHIJKLMNO
XYZ 1234567890 123456

Palatino

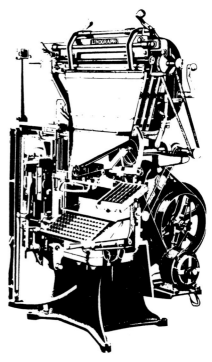

Linograph Model 3

adaptation of a linecasting machine to phototypesetting. Matrices were fitted with characters in the form of photographic negatives or positives. Assembly and distribution of the matrices adhered to the well-established principles of circulation, but the molten metal and casting apparatus was replaced by camera equipment. Line justification relied upon the proven method of opposing wedges. Photography of a composed line of matrices was by transmitted light (see 1926).

1922

LIN   Linotype Model 6 built in Britain, the machine held four magazines and permitted mixing in three combinations (i.e. two upper, two centre, and two lower), instead of only in two combinations as on the Linotype Model 65 (see 1913).

LIN   American Court upheld a complaint by the Lanston Monotype Machine Company that the Elrod Lead and Rule Caster infringed its patent 7202 of 1915. In Britain the London Express Newspaper Ltd. agreed to pay the Lanston Monotype Corporation Ltd. royalties for continued use of the Elrod machine. The dispute was settled more formally in 1925 between the two principal companies.

TYP   Stanley Morison appointed Typographic Adviser to the Monotype Corporation, an association invoking the issue of a remarkable collection of typefaces. Many were based on historical precedents as researched by Morison. Others resulted from innovative design exercises.

TYP   First design in the programme of typographic development conceived by Stanley Morison for the Monotype Corporation was issued, namely Garamond Series 156. More than 10,000 sets of hot-metal matrices of the design had been sold by the 1980s.

J&P   Harvard University Press published the two volumes on *Printing Types* by D. B. Updike, the founder of the Merrymount Press in 1893. Text for the books was based on university lectures delivered between 1911 and 1916.

PTS   Walter Broadbent obtained a patent for a phototypesetting machine. It proposed the use of an adapted Monotype keyboard for producing a control tape which activated pneumatically-operated shutters in the exposure unit for character selection. Every character in the photo-matrix array had a dedicated focusing lens, shutter, and prism which deflected images to a common exposure point. Character spacing was to be accomplished by movement of the photo-sensitive material.

abcdefghijklmnopqrstuv
ABCDEFGHIJKLMN
XYZ 1234567890 12345

Garamond

1923

LIN   Single power-driven keyboard announced for Linotype machine. It incorporated a keybutton shift control permitting the alternate assembly of matrices from main and side magazines. Hitherto access to a side magazine had necessitated the use of a discrete auxiliary keyboard which tended to interrupt operational flow.

LIN   Linotype Model 4SM built in Britain. It was configured with three main magazines and two side magazines.

LIN   Linotype Model 4SM used for composing a full character complement of the Arabic script. It was enabled by the employment of a 90-channel main magazine augmented by a side magazine.

MON   Lanston Monotype Machine Company in the USA announced the Monotype Material Maker, a unit for casting sorts, leads, rules, and other composing-room materials. It did not compose type and must have given rise later to development of the Super Caster in Britain (see 1928).

MC   Linograph with an unprecedented dozen magazines of 90 channels apiece entered the market. It offered a size range from 5 to 24 point and from 30 to 60 point in condensed type designs.

TF   Stephenson, Blake & Co. Ltd. started to produce composing cabinets in steel.

TYP   Baskerville Series 169 typeface cut by the Monotype Corporation. More than 20,000 sets of hot metal matrices of the design had been sold by the 1980s gaining third ranking in Monotype popularity after Times New Roman (see 1932) and Old Style No. 2.

TYP   Poliphilus Series 170 typeface launched by the Monotype Corporation. It was based on a Venetian fifteenth-century model used by Aldus Manutius.

TYP   First publication emerged from the Officina Bodoni of Giovanni Mardersteig, the designer of several typefaces instanced by Griffo (1930), Zeno (1936), and most notably Dante (1954). In 1936 Mardersteig designed the Fontana type for the publisher Collins.

J&P   *The Fleuron: a Journal of Typography* appeared for the first time. It ran to seven issues through to 1930. Oliver Simon edited the initial four numbers printed at the Curwen Press, while Stanley Morison edited the last three numbers produced at the Cambridge University Press. Arousal by the magazine of typographic consciousness was considerable.

TF   Edward Prince, the punchcutter, died on 2 December. He was responsible for the cutting of a number of type founts, notably: the Golden, Troy and Chaucer types for William Morris at the Kelmscott Press in 1890, 1891 and 1892 respectively; the Doves Press type in 1900; and the Subiaco type of the Ashendene Press in 1901. More than 70 founts are traceable to the interpretative hands of Edward Prince. He has been described as 'the last regular independent punchcutter in England'.

1924

LIN   Linotype Models 25 and 26 released. They replaced the Models 16 and 17 of 1916.

LIN   Linotype Parts Co. formed in New York to import and to sell spares for Linotype and eventually for Intertype machines as well. Its name changed some three decades later to the Star Parts Co.

MON   First Monotype units manufactured entirely in Britain were marketed.

MON   Dotted rule mould perfected for the Monotype Caster.

TF   Deberny & Peignot typefoundry formed from an amalgamation of two companies: Girard & Cie set up by Alexandre Deberny and the Peignot foundry established by Gustave Peignot.

TO   Double Crown Club founded by Oliver Simon, Holbrook Jackson, and Hubert Foss. It is a dining club for eminent typographers, printers, publishers, bibliophiles, and others concerned with quality printing.

1925

LIN   M. H. Whittaker & Son Ltd. designed and introduced the Mickey Mouse linecaster, a machine intended for producing display lines from hand-assembled matrices. It was fashioned on a Star-Base Linotype Model 1.

MON   Extended die-case introduced for Monotype machines which bolstered the number of individual matrices (or typographic characters) accommodated from 225 to 255 arranged in a grid of 15 x 17 rows, instead of 15 x 15 as previously.

MON   Three-unit justification space attachment engineered for Monotype machines. It encouraged and enabled the closer spacing of text.

MON   Extension of maximum line length devised for the Monotype system as the 90-em attachment.

TYP   Mergenthaler Linotype Co. introduced the Ionic typeface for newspaper composition. Within 18 months of release, the design had been adopted by 3,000 publications. In the United Kingdom, the fashion for Ionic was started by the *Daily Herald* during 1930. The

abcdefghijklmnopqrstu
ABCDEFGHIJKLMN
YZ 1234567890 12345

Baskerville

ABCDEFGHIJKL
abcdefghijklmno

Dante

abcdefghijklmnopqr
ABCDEFGHIJKLM
WXYZ 1234567890

Ionic

development stimulated a whole new series of newspaper types now known as the Legibility Group. Ionic was based on nineteenth-century slab-serifed, monotone Egyptians of British origin.

TYP   Fournier Series 185 typeface first marketed by the Monotype Corporation. It was based on an eighteenth-century French model. Demand for the design by printers was not particularly strong and less than 650 sets of hot-metal matrices had been sold by the 1980s.

TYP   Herbert Bayer established a typography workshop at the Bauhaus school in Dessau under Walter Gropius. It developed a fresh concept of functionalism in typography characterised by assymetric page layouts and by the use of sanserif letter forms. He went on to create the Bayer Type for Berthold in 1935 and to design several typographic promotional items for the same typefoundry.

SO   The Typary machine was launched at the Printing Exhibition in London. It was a composing and reproduction proofing system of Swiss design and marketed in Britain by the Typary & Typon Company Ltd. from an address just off Fleet Street. Lowe and Brydone did use the device for a short time to compose books for offset-lithographic printing. One title published was *Keeping Well*. Characters in the machine consisted of patrices with raised images. Groups of letters sharing a common width were mounted on type bars. Keyboard operation caused the type bars to drop bringing the required characters to a 'print' level ready for transport to an assembly point. Justification took place and the line of patrices was inked and impressed on to Baryta paper. Automatic distribution of the type bars ensued and the paper was moved on the correct amount to accommodate the next line.

PTS   R. J. Smothers proposed the conversion of a slug-casting machine for phototypesetting. In essence the idea was similar to that of Robertson, Brown and Orrel (see 1921) and involved the photography by transmitted light of a complete line of assembled matrices. It contrasted with the scheme of Friedman and Bloom (see 1926) which involved the use of reflective light.

1926

LIN   Linotype Model 6SM built in Britain. Equipment configuration consisted of four main magazines and four side magazines.

LIN   Walter W. Morey conceived the teletypesetter process whereby linecasting machines could be operated from 6-level (originally 5-level) punched paper tape produced at off-line keyboards. Commercial application did not occur for six years.

MON   Monotype Giant Caster unveiled in the USA. It was designed to cast sorts from 18 to 72 point. When fitted with appropriate moulds, the same unit could cast strip materials, including furniture.

MON   Temperature regulators introduced for the control of metal pots on Monotype machines.

TF   Melvin Cary established the Continental Type Foundry in New York for the purpose of importing European types into the USA.

MON   Lord Dunraven, Chairman of the Monotype Corporation Ltd. since its inception in 1897, died on 14 June.

PTS   The term *photocomposing* for reference to the processes of photographic typesetting dates from about this time as seen in *The Penrose Annual*. It was subsequently avoided because of confusion in American usage with the same word describing step-and-repeat exposures on to printing plates.

PTS   In New York Samuel Friedman and Dr. Otto Bloom suggested the adaptation of a linecaster for phototypesetting. Mounted in the narrow edges of the matrices were white opaque characters on black backgrounds. Keyboard assembly and mechanical distribution of characters took place in traditional fashion. Once composed, the line of matrices was photographed by reflected light (see 1921 and 1925).

Earl of Dunraven

SO   George Eaton Hart, of the St. Clements Press, secured a patent for a composing and reproduction proofing machine. Essentially the idea proposed the conversion of a linecaster. Instead of the usual matrices circulating around the system, the invention called for the employment of patrices with letters in relief. Substituted for the customary metal pot and casting apparatus was a proofing unit. Accordingly the patrices were assembled into lines from a keyboard, justified to a measure mechanically, inked, and impressed on to paper. Afterwards the patrices were distributed automatically back into their storage magazines. It was a notion to be resurrected in the Orotype machine (see 1937).

1927

LIN   M. H. Whittaker & Son Ltd. took out an early patent (No. 291544) for automatic centring of copy on a linecaster.

LIN   Feasibility model of a teletypesetter perforator was built.

TYP   Paul Renner (1878–1956) designed the Futura geometric sanserif typeface for the Bauer foundry. It was exceedingly popular at the time and has undergone vigorous revival in recent years.

TYP   Formation of the Society of Typographic Arts in Chicago.

J&P   *L & M News* launched as an external house magazine for the Linotype Group of Companies in Britain. It has carried over the years many influential articles by industrial notables.

1928

LIN   Initial public demonstration of the teletypesetter system took place at the Times Union Building in Rochester, New York. Both Linotype and Intertype machines featured in the showing along with the two components of a teletypesetting system, namely a tape perforating keyboard and an operating unit or tape reader.

MON   Functioning as a complete typefoundry, the Monotype Super Caster was promoted in the United Kingdom. It output the various materials needed in a hand composing department, such as founts of type, quads, quotations, furniture, leads, and rules. No keyboard was required to work the Super Caster.

TYP   British Typographers Guild established by Vincent Steer, Alfred Vernon, Edward Burrett, and others. In 1953 the name changed to the Society of Typographic Designers.

J&P   Jan Tschichold published the book *Die neue Typographie*. It enshrined the philosophy of the modern typography movement which eschewed decoration, adhered strictly to functionality, purported to express the spirit of the machine age, espoused purity and simplicity, embraced assymetry, and spoke in sanserif types.

1929

LIN   New keyboard integrated into Linotype machine which swung outwards from the main body and enabled access for speedy servicing. Previously keyboards had to be completely disembodied from the machine and removed to a workbench for repair.

LIN   Fresh design of side magazine developed for the Linotype machine. It was wider and accommodated 34 channels: a half-dozen more than previous comparable units. Machines could be equipped with up to three of the new magazines capable of running matrices for type not exceeding 36 point.

LIN   Teletypesetter Corporation formed. Experimental TTS installation undertaken at the *News Index* in Evanston, Illinois.

TF   Lanston Monotype Company bought the Thompson Type Machine Company and obtained rights to the sorts caster made by that organisation. In the USA the machine continued in production until

abcdefghijklmnopqrstuv
ABCDEFGHIJKLMNOP
1234567890 .,;:"«»&!?

Futura

Monotype Super Caster

the early 1960s and was withdrawn from the product line in the United Kingdom during 1967.

LIN Electrical heater developed for the crucible on an Elrod machine. Previously gas-heated pots had been supplied.

TYP Bembo Series 270 typeface promoted by the Monotype Corporation. It was based on an Aldine roman of the fifteenth century. More than 6,800 sets of hot-metal matrices of the design had been sold by the 1980s.

J&P Limited Editions Club founded in New York by George Macy with the aim of issuing fine books for discriminating collectors.

ABCDEFGHIJKL
abcdefghijklmnop
Bembo

1930

LIN Intertype Model F revealed in the USA. It was a two-magazine mixing machine using a single-distributor box.

TYP Bell Series 341 typeface cut by the Monotype Corporation. It was based on an eighteenth-century British model. Demand by printers for the design was reticent as evidenced by only 300 sets of hot-metal matrices having been sold by the 1980s.

TYP Emery Walker knighted for services to printing.

TYP Society of Industrial Artists and Designers was formed.

PTS Several British patents were issued to Edmund Uher for a phototypesetting system. Two schemes were envisaged in a variety of proposals. They were a keyboard-operated text system and a manually-operated photolettering system (see 1938). In the former, a perforated paper tape provided input to an exposure unit containing a glass photo-matrix cylinder which rotated in response to incoming signals. Characters were imaged in lines end-to-end on a narrow band of photosensitive material. After chemical processing, the band was cut up into text lines for assembly as a galley.

ABCDEFGHIJ
abcdefghijklmno
Bell

1931

LIN Mechanical thermostat conceived for regulating the heat of the electric metal pot on the Linotype machine.

LIN Automatic quadding and centring device developed for Intertype machines, an advance emulated on Linotype equipment in 1932.

MON Name of the Lanston Monotype Corporation changed to The Monotype Corporation Limited.

PTS Early use of the term *phototypesetting* occurred in *ASME News*.

TYP Ayer Award for Excellence in Newspaper Typography inaugurated in the USA.

1932

LIN Two-in-One Linotype machines released. Essentially the structure of the units accommodated magazines with 90 and 72 channels for running text and display matrices and incorporated two separate distributor bars and sets of channel entrances. The name two-in-one was intended to conjure the notion of a linecaster able to produce integrated body text and display matter.

LIN All-Purpose Linotype machine launched. It cast slugs from 5 to 144 point from matrices assembled by hand in special sticks. Maximum line length was 42 picas and the biggest body size 72 point. The largest faces cast in the machine overhung the body

LIN Automatic self-quadding mechanism added to Linotype machine. It quadded lines to the left, right, or centre automatically by manipulating the vice jaws as appropriate on operator command. Blank or white lines could be cast using the same mechanism and without composing any matrices. Essentially the mechanism increased production by eliminating the assembly of fixed space matrices and spacebands formerly needed to fill out quadded lines (see 1906).

LIN   Magazines made from a light alloy instituted for Linotype machines. Known as Linolite, the new incarnation of the 90-channel magazine weighed 22 pounds less than the forerunning brass equivalent. It reduced exertion of the operator at machine changeovers.

LIN   Intertype Model G machine surfaced in the USA for text and display composition. It held two magazines. One had 90 channels and the other 72.

LIN   Teletypesetter (TTS) equipment made available commercially using unit-cut matrices only.

MON   Copy repeating attachment launched for the Monotype system.

MON   Automatic leading attachment conceived for the Monotype Caster.

TYP   Times New Roman developed for setting the editorial columns of *The Times* newspaper in London. Produced under the direction of Stanley Morison and drawn by Victor Lardent, the new type design has been regarded by many as a 'modernised Plantin'. First issue of the newspaper to appear in the fresh typographic dress emerged on 3 October. In 1933 the type became generally available to the printing industry on linecasting and Monotype machines and grew to be ubiquitous.

TYP   London & North Eastern Railway adopted the typeface Gill Sans as a house style.

TF   Linn Boyd Benton died. He was the inventor in 1885 of a mechanical and pantographic punchcutting machine which made the batch production of metal matrices feasible. In the absence of the development, the progress of mechanical composition (with its necessity for multiple matrices) would have been impossible.

KEY   August Dvorak proposed a fresh layout of keybuttons for the standard typewriter. Disposition of characters was based on a great deal of text analysis, the intent being to provide a more equal distribution of labour between the two hands and to allot characters of high-frequency to the stronger fingers. Occasionally the manufacturers of composition systems flirt with the Dvorak keyboard and usually without noticeable or permanent effect.

1933

LIN   Power-assisted shifting of matrix magazines developed for the Linotype machine. It facilitated operation, especially on mixed compositions.

LIN   Intertype Model H introduced with three 72-channel magazines for display composition.

LIN   Composing stick attachment developed for Intertype machines. It enabled slugs to be cast from hand-assembled matrices for type sizes up to 60 point.

LIN   Special rule-form matrices conceived for the Ludlow machine. Perfect alignment of vertical rules on the resultant slugs arose from a simple interlocking by tongue and socket.

SO   Ralph C. Coxhead bought rights to the Varityper strike-on machine for $100,000 from the bankrupt Hepburn Company.

TYP   Robert Hunter Middleton appointed Director of Type Design for the Ludlow Typograph Co. He had joined the firm ten years earlier in 1923. His letter designs include Eusebius (1924), Record Gothic (1927), Delphian (1928), Stellar (1929), Tempo (1930), Karnak (1931), Radiant (1938), and Florentine (1956).

TYP   Jan Tschichold designed several typefaces for the Uhertype photosetting machine (see 1930). Unfortunately a record of the work has not survived.

TYP   Sir Emery Walker died on 22 July.

TYP   In New York a luncheon club for typographic enthusiasts formed under the name of The Typophiles. Several enchanting and significant printed keepsakes have been issued by the group.

PTS   General Printing Ink Co. of New York obtained a patent for a

abcdefghijklmnopqrstuv
ABCDEFGHIJKLMNO
1234567890 1234567890

Times

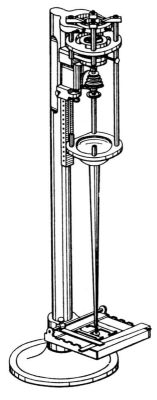

**Punchcutting machine of
Linn Boyd Benton**

photolettering machine which was to be developed and manufactured by its Rutherford Machinery Division. Ashley Ogden had the original idea for the device which was sold to the General Printing Ink Co. in 1931. Several people perfected and persisted with the concept, notably Harold Horman and Ed Rondthaler. In essence the machine encompassed a photo-matrix slide which was moved manually to sandwich a selected character between a light source above and a projection lens below. Inter-character spacing was conducted visually by the operator shifting laterally the lens and lamp assembly. Visual control under darkroom conditions was aided by intercepting the optical path with a periscope arrangement which displayed the positioning of characters to the operator without fogging the photosensitive ouput material.

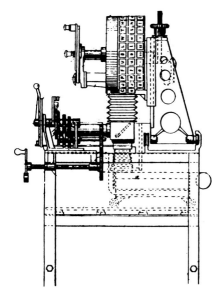

Rutherford Photolettering Machine

1934

LIN   Design of universal knife block (see 1909) on Linotype machine enhanced for rigidity and precision.

LIN   Installation of first teletypesetter-operated linecasters in Europe at *The Scotsman* newspaper. Intertype F mixer machines were involved, as well as data transmissions between Edinburgh and London.

LIN   Development commenced of a Teletypesetter Multiface Perforator which could count non-unit matrices. Removable counting magazines were devised for the keyboard. Such a development widened the potential applications of TTS to general commercial printing as well as to newspapers.

TYP   Walbaum Series 374 typeface first marketed by the Monotype Corporation. More than 1,200 sets of hot-metal matrices of the design had been sold by the 1980s.

TYP   Rudolf Koch, the celebrated German calligrapher and letter designer, died on 9 April. He was associated with the Klingspor typefoundry from 1906 until the end of his life. Typefaces attributable to him include: Maximilian Antiqua (1914), Koch Antiqua (1922), Neuland (1923), Wallau (1925), Kabel (1927), Prisma (1928), Jessen (1930), Marathon (1931), Holla (1932), and Offenbach (1935).

TYP   The Monotype Corporation Limited released the winsome and original Albertus type design by Berthold Wolpe.

MC   John R. Rogers, inventor of the Typograph machine (see 1890), died.

J&P   First edition appeared of the book *Type Designs: their History and Development* by A. F. Johnson.

J&P   Vincent Steer had published the book *Printing Design and Layout* which did much to improve the status of the typographic designer in Britain. Some 18,000 copies were sold up to the year 1958.

abcdefghijklmnopqrs
ABCDEFGHIJKLMNO
XYZ 1234567890 .,;:'"«

Walbaum

ABCDEFGHIJK
abcdefghijklmn

Albertus

1935

LIN   Development of split magazine concept (see 1918) for Linotype machine occurred with the emergence of the three-quarter magazine. Split magazines ran 12 matrices in 90 channels and 10 matrices in 72 channels; whereas the three-quarter innovation had a capacity for 16 matrices irrespective of the channel configuration.

LIN   Widened super-display magazine inaugurated for Linotype machine. It accommodated matrices for type sizes up to 36 point and contained 72 channels.

LIN   Duplex display matrices inaugurated on Linotype machines for type sizes 18 and 24 point. Previously the upper limit for two-letter matrices had been 14 point.

LIN   First Linotype machine, a Model 6, was operated from punched paper tape input at *The Scotsman* newspaper (see 1934).

LIN   Low-quadding device perfected for Intertype machines.

TF   Louis Hoell, the punchcutter, died in Frankfurt. He cut faces for the Bauer and Flinsch foundries.

J&P   *Signature,* a periodical dedicated to typography and the graphic arts, commenced publication under the editorship of Oliver Simon. Fifteen issues appeared up to 1940 and a New Series resumed after the second world war comprising eighteen issues between the years 1946 and 1954. It was a discriminating and influential publication.

PTS   *The Penrose Annual* contained a specimen page setting from the hand-operated Uhertype photolettering machine.

PTS   Booklet released of specimens set on the hand-operated Uhertype photocomposition system. The work was designed by Imre Reiner and demonstrated the freedom in job layout allowed by the new medium (see 1930).

1936

LIN   Smallest type size obtainable from a Linotype machine reduced to 4 point.

LIN   Wheel holding six moulds promoted for Linotype machine.

LIN   International Printing Exhibition staged in the United Kingdom. It prompted Linotype & Machinery Ltd. to show five novel linecasters, namely: Model 48, Model 48SM, Model 50, Model 50SM, and Super-Range.

LIN   Four-magazine versions of the Intertype Models F, G, and H emerged.

SO   Automatic line justification introduced to the Varityper strike-on machine.

J&P   Stanley Morison's milestone essay on the *First Principles of Typography* published by the Cambridge University Press. It had appeared previously in a somewhat different version as part of the *Encyclopedia Britannica* (1929) and of *The Fleuron* (1930).

J&P   *Typography,* a quarterly publication, launched under the editorship of Robert Harling from the Shenval Press at Hertford. Eight issues constituted the series which ended in 1939.

PTS   George Westover filed for patent protection of the Rotofoto system of photographic type composition. Four units constituted the proposals: a standard Monotype keyboard produced a 31-channel spool for the control of the line projector (i.e. a Monotype caster adapted for photography) which exposed text on to 35mm. film. Completing the system were a proof projector and a page projector. Several far-sighted and revolutionary ideas were embraced, notably the assembly of pages and the blending of correction lines into a body of text by optical projection. Many other issues ignored by previous inventors were addressed. Despite writings to the contrary, the development of the Rotofoto system was quite separate and distinct from that of the Monophoto Filmsetter.

PTS   Photo-Lettering Inc. was formed in New York by Ed Rondthaler and others as a subsidiary of the Electrographic Corporation. It provided an early service to advertising agencies and design studios of photocomposed display work. Equipment used was the Rutherford Photo-Letter Composing Machine (see 1933).

1937

LIN   Linotype Models 31 and 32 released in the USA, the machines were equivalent respectively to the British-built Linotype Models 48 and 48SM.

LIN   Two-letter matrices for type sizes 18 and 24 point introduced for Intertype machines.

MON   Automatic quadding and centreing attachment incorporated in the Monotype system.

TYP   Ehrhardt Series 453 cut by the Monotype Corporation. It is based on a seventeenth-century continental European model. Nearly 1,000 sets of hot-metal matrices of the design had been sold by the 1980s.

TF   H. W. Caslon & Co. Ltd. acquired by Stephenson, Blake & Co. Ltd.,

abcdefghijklmnopqrstuv
ABCDEFGHIJKLMN
XYZ 1234567890 12345

Ehrhardt

thereby continuing concentration of the British typefounding industry.

SO   *The Penrose Annual* contained a complete article by R. B. Fishenden dedicated to, and set on, the Orotype machine. It was an outgrowth of the earlier Typary device (see 1925) which had been used among others by Lowe & Brydone and by J. Ullmann GmbH at Zwickau. Though sound in principle, the Typary suffered from detailed design defects primarily associated with the type bar assembly mechanism. As a result of the experience gained, the Orotype was developed and remained a composing and reproduction proofing machine. In appearance the unit resembled a linecaster (the Typary did not) and used characters in the form of circulating patrices. In place of the casting mechanism, a proofing sub-assembly was substituted. Manufacturer of the Orotype was the Swiss Locomotive and Machine Works in Winterthur, though much of the development impetus and activity emanated from Dr. Max Ullmann.

1938

LIN   Intertype Model G with double distributor emerged in the United Kingdom.

MC   Linograph Model 50 announced with five vertical magazines of matrices and embodying a short second elevator for the first time. Standard linecaster matrices were introduced (see 1912).

MON   Combined spacing attachment released for the Monotype system whereby the justified spaces were cast integrally with the first letters of every word. Some 16 per cent of casting time was saved by the technique.

TYP   Bell Gothic, a condensed sanserif type, issued in the USA by the Bell Telephone organisation for setting directories and market prices. It was cut by the Mergenthaler Linotype Co.

PTS   Waterlow & Sons Ltd. of Dunstable produced a booklet entitled *Typesetting Methods: Old and New* on the hand-operated version of the Uhertype machine (see 1930). Three machines constituted the system: a setting unit, a line justifying unit, and a make-up unit. The setting unit employed a photo-matrix grid which was moved manually to bring selected characters to an exposure point. At the end of each text line, the deficit of space was noted as a guide to setting up the justifying unit. After processing, the resulting roll film was input to the justifying unit for the individual words to be projected consecutively on to another piece of film, the space separating them being adjusted by the mechanism automatically. Optical merging of corrections was also performed at this stage. Finally the make-up of a job could be accomplished by optical projection on the third unit known as the Metteur machine. Manufacturer of the Uhertype system was M.A.N.

abcdefghijklmnopqrstuvw
ABCDEFGHIJKLMNOP
1234567890 .,;:'`«»&!?

Bell Gothic

1939

LIN   Thermo-Blo mould cooler made available on the Linotype machine. It generated a frigid air flow for cooling the mould cap and proved to be a successful refinement of linecasting. Previous attempts at water cooling had been a failure. Air cooling enabled faster casting speeds to be contemplated and vouchsafed the quality of slugs.

LIN   New heating elements and temperature controls introduced for the electric metal pot on the Linotype machine. The new system afforded better heat distribution and more responsive control, both to the crucible and to the throat and mouthpiece of the casting area. Lino-Therm was the adopted tradename.

TYP   Death occurred of Frederic Warde, the American book designer and typographer. He designed Arrighi Italic which was cut by Plumet in Paris during 1925 and subsequently by the Monotype Corporation during 1929. The latter effort served to accompany the Centaur roman of Bruce Rogers. His writings include *Printers Ornaments* published by the Monotype Corporation during 1928.

PTS   William C. Huebner patented a phototypesetting machine. It stored type styles around a stationary photo-matrix disc. Associated with each character was a complete optical projection unit comprising a light source, a lens, a shutter, and reflecting mirrors. Both keyboard and tape operation of the machine was envisaged as alternatives, a call for a character causing the desired image to be projected and photographed.

1940

TYP   Eric Gill died on 17 November. His type designs encompassed Perpetua (1928), Gill Sans (1929), Solus (1929), Aries (1932), Bunyan (1934), Jubilee (1935), and Joanna (1937). In addition to type designing, Eric Gill had many other accomplishments. He was a brilliant illustrative wood-engraver as manifest in countless books, a gifted sculptor, and wrote an individualistic and notable *Essay on Typography* published in 1931.

1941

MON   On 10 May the Monotype offices in London at 43 Fetter Lane were destroyed by bombing.

1942

LIN   Linotype Auto-Ejector developed: a time-saving device that protected liners and moulds against wrongly-set ejector blades.

TYP   Daniel B. Updike, the respected American printer, died (see 1922).

TYP   Emil R. Weiss died. He taught graphic art in Berlin and designed a few typefaces initially for the Bauer foundry, exemplified by Weiss Roman (1926) and Weiss Rundgotisch (1936).

TO   Book Production War Economy Agreement invoked. It established minimum specifications to prevent wastage, such as type area not less than 58 per cent of the page and dictated maximum point sizes for given formats.

1944

LIN   Linograph Corporation taken over in January by the Intertype Corporation.

TYP   Edward Johnston, the calligrapher, died on 26 November. He was involved to varying degrees in a few type design projects, notably that for *The Imprint* magazine (see 1912) and that for the Cranach Press of Count Kessler.

PTS   The Monotype Corporation Ltd. commenced research on the project that eventually surfaced as the Monophoto filmsetter.

1945

J&P   Stanley Morison appointed editor of *The Times Literary Supplement*.

PTS   Rene Higonnet and Louis Moyroud established the principle of stroboscopically selecting and imaging characters from a fount arrayed around a continuously spinning photo-matrix disc. It was a method that enabled a multiplicity of characters to be stored compactly and accessed rapidly without the mechanical complications attaching to alternative techniques. During this year the flash feasibility model was completed, though commercial application did not occur until the middle 1950s.

PTS   Chester F. Carlson formulated the basic principles of xerography and

Portrait of Eric Gill

abcdefghijklmnopqrstuvw
ABCDEFGHIJKLMNOPQ
1234567890 .,;:'"«»&!?

Gill Sans

xeroprinting in American patents. Development of the concepts was conducted by the Battelle Memorial Institute.

1946

PTS US Government Printing Office in Washington became the successful test site for an Intertype Fotosetter which proved to be the first phototypesetting machine to endure in a commercial environment. It was a system imitative of hot-metal techniques and had much outward resemblance to a linecaster. Indeed many of the basic functional principles of linecasting were preserved, such as the direct keyboard operation of the machine and the deployment of recirculating individual matrices.

PTS Pamphlet of 16 pages devoted to the *National Gallery of Art, Washington DC* was set on the Intertype Fotosetter at the Government Printing Office.

PTS Prototype of the Higonnet-Moyroud phototypesetting machine (see 1945) was demonstrated privately in the USA to Bill Garth of the Lithomat Corporation, to Professor Samuel Caldwell of the Massachusetts Institute of Technology, and to a patent attorney. Seemingly the event was a success and the machine received endorsement within a couple of months and a development contract ensued.

PTS Walter Peery began experimentation with phototypesetting (see 1952).

CAT First electronic calculator or computer invented by J. P. Eckert and J. W. Maunchly, the system was known by the acronym ENIAC standing for Electronic Numerical Integrator and Calculator. It contained 18,000 valves and was used initially for computing missile trajectories.

1947

SO Differentially-spaced characters incorporated in the Varityper strike-on machine.

SO The *Chicago Tribune* newspaper was set by editorial staff on Varityper strike-on machines because of a dispute with compositors in membership of the International Typographical Union which precluded the use of conventional hot-metal linecasters.

TYP Frederic Goudy, the prolific American typographer, died on 11 May. His type design credits embrace Pabst Roman (1902), Kennerley (1911), Forum Capitals (1912), Goudy Old Style (1915), Goudy Modern (1918), and Hadriano (1918). He was consultant to the Lanston Monotype Company and ran the Village Press.

TYP Walter Tracy joined the Linotype Group of Companies in a part-time capacity which became full-time two years later. His type designs include Jubilee (1953), Adsans (1959), Maximus (1967), Linotype Modern (for the *Daily Telegraph* 1969), and Times Europa (1972). Other notable work has encompassed the design of exotic scripts, particularly several Arabic styles. In 1973 Walter Tracy received the award Royal Designer for Industry from the Royal Society of Arts. He has written extensively and incisively on typographic subjects, notably the book *Letters of Credit* published in 1986.

1948

PTS Rotofoto system (see 1936) demonstrated for the first time in public at the newly-opened Leatherhead offices of the Printing, Packaging and Allied Trades Research Association (the antecedent of PIRA) on 28 October; an event that received notice in *The Times* of 2 November. PATRA issued an *Information Leaflet No. 32* to apprise members of *Photo-Typesetting: a description of the Rotofoto System.*

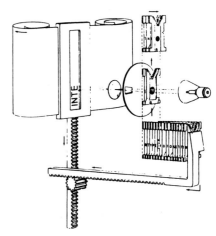

Optical system for the Fotosetter

Caricature of Frederic Goudy

abcdefghijklmnopqr
ABCDEFGHIJKLM
XYZ 1234567890 .,;:'

Linotype Modern

The installation at Leatherhead was temporary and lasted for a couple of months. Manufacture of the equipment was undertaken by the Coventry Gauge and Tool Co. Ltd. Soon afterwards a system was installed at the London School of Printing. Other machines were installed by Mondadori in Verona and by the South African Government Printing Office in Pretoria.

PTS Initial installation of a Hadego phototypesetting machine occurred. Contemporary writers frequently alluded to the device as the 'photographic Ludlow'. Inventor of the system was Dr. H. J. A. de Goeij of Overseen in the Netherlands. Machines were made by NV Exploitatiemaatschappij of Amsterdam and marketed by NV Quod Bonum of Haarlem. Hadego matrices comprised individual plastic blocks with white letters on a black ground. Assembly and justification of the matrices was conducted by hand in a proprietary composing stick which on completion of a line was mounted in front of a camera sub-assembly for photographing by reflected light. Included in the equipment was a circular slide rule for setting degrees of enlargement and reduction. Area composition was feasible on the machine.

PTS Prototype of the Higonnet-Moyroud phototypesetting machine (see 1946) was completed and imported to the USA on 15 July, the same day that the two French inventors immigrated to the country.

1949

PTS Booklet of sixteen pages entitled *Rotofoto* was produced at the London School of Printing (see 1948) on the subject machine under the direction of H. O. Smith, a great proselytiser of the new technology. Inserted in the booklet was a separate slip that detailed the operational times and proudly pointed out that the 35mm. films for the sixteen pages weighed an ounce, whereas the metal type equivalent would have been 0.75 hundredweight! From the standpoint of bibliographers, the *Rotofoto* booklet is of enormous significance as the earliest phototypeset publication to be produced in Europe on a keyboard-operated system.

PTS Pre-production model of the Higonnet-Moyroud phototypesetting machine demonstrated at the Waldorf Astoria Hotel in New York during April.

PTS Bill Garth established the Graphic Arts Research Foundation (GARF) to sponsor the developments of Higonnet and Moyroud in the field of phototypesetting.

PTS Optical character escapement carriage for Photon machines invented by Dr. Samuel Caldwell of the Massachusetts Institute of Technology (see 1945 and 1946). It avoided the more taxing movement of the photo-sensitive material.

PTS R. Hoe & Crabtree Ltd. appointed distributor for the Rotofoto system: a commercial liaison doomed to failure.

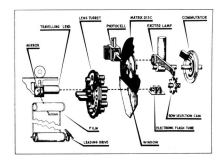

Optical system of the first Higonnet-Moyroud phototypesetter (including the Caldwell escapement)

1950

PTS Linotype Group of Companies adopted the notion of Friedman and Bloom (see 1926) to convert a linecasting machine for phototypesetting purposes. It was used internally and experimentally, but quickly abandoned as inappropriate to modern needs. As Ted Emery of Linotype once remarked, 'the use of a ton and a half of casting machinery to manipulate beams of light was not the correct approach'.

SO Justowriter strike-on composition system launched by Commercial Controls. Friden later took over the system which devolved in 1963 to the Singer Manufacturing Co. The equipment provided the blueprint for development of the ATF Typesetter (see 1958 and 1970).

TF Dr. Karl Klingspor died on 1 January (see 1892).

PTS Experimental version of the Monophoto filmsetter was demonstrated on a controlled basis (see 1952).

1951

LIN American press associations began to transmit justified teletypesetter tapes to subscribing newspapers. By the end of 1952 some 400 daily newspapers were receiving the service. Standardised unit-cut matrices were crucial to the diffuse operations.

SO Ralph C. Coxhead, the man who made the Varityper strike-on machine a success, died.

TYP Walter Tiemann died. He taught at the Staatliche Akademie der Graphischen Kunste in Leipzig and designed a number of typefaces for the Klingspor typefoundry, instanced by Tiemann Mediaeval (1909), Tiemann (1923), Orpheus (1928), Daphnis (1931), and Offizin (released posthumously in 1952).

abcdefghijklmnopqrstuvw
ABCDEFGHIJKLMNO
1234567890 .,;:'"«»&!?

Tiemann

1952

SO Varityper Headliner Photo-Composing Machine launched. It contact-printed characters by exposure to photo-sensitive material from a manually-rotated photo-matrix disc and produced excellent output quality.

TF Miller & Richard typefoundry closed.

PTS The Rotofoto system at the London School of Printing (see 1948 and 1949) was used to compose the booklet *This Thing Called Rotofoto: some notes for young inventors* by George Westover. As a piece of writing the text displays great clarity and constitutes an elegantly reasoned statement of the difficulties confronted by engineers in designing a phototypesetting machine.

PTS H. O. Smith lectured on phototypesetting to the Guild of Printing Trades Executives and supported the precepts enunciated by a practical exemplar in the form of a booklet called *Photo-Composition and Make-Up by the Rotofoto Process*. It was produced at the London School of Printing on the subject equipment.

PTS *Handbook of Basic Microtechnique* by Peter Gray was composed on the Intertype Fotosetter. It was published by the Blakiston Company and arguably constitutes the first phototypeset book in the USA.

PTS E. Silcock, the general manager of The Monotype Corporation Ltd. wrote in *The Penrose Annual* that the Monophoto machine had 'emerged from years of testing and development to the level where it can now be placed into commercial operation'.

PTS Photon Inc. was established to manufacture phototypesetting machines based on the inventions of Higonnet and Moyroud and as sponsored to date by the Graphic Arts Research Foundation.

PTS Time Inc. withdrew financial support from the development work of Walter Peery. Many interesting concepts were embodied in the Peery Photographic Typecomposing System, the most novel being the use of a rotating mirror for character escapement which found initial commercial expression in the machines of Berthold (Diatronic) and Fairchild (PTS 2000) of 1967.

1953

LIN High-Speed Model C Intertype linecaster introduced at the British Industries Fair. Production was rated at 10 to 12 newspaper lines per minute. Teletypesetter tape operation was primarily envisaged, but the machine could be operated manually from an integral keyboard.

PTS Intertype Ltd. in the United Kingdom installed a Fotosetter machine for demonstration purposes.

PTS First book composed on the Higonnet-Moyroud phototypesetting system was published by Reinhardt & Co. Inc. in the USA. Entitled

The Wonderful World of Insects by Albro T. Gaul, the volume was set in a version of Scotch Roman and printed by letterpress from powderless-etched magnesium plates. Though published in 1953, the book was composed in the preceding year.

PTS   *La Disfatta,* a novel by Alfredo Oriani, produced on the Rotofoto system by Mondadori in Verona.

PTS   *Shakespeare and the Welfare State* by Max Reese, a booklet Rotofoto set at the London School of Printing, was produced as a handout to reinforce a lecture given by H. O. Smith to the Congress of the British Federation of Master Printers. Over 400 delegates attended and the proselytising of the speaker induced considerable reaction and was a landmark in the history of phototypesetting. Demand for copies of the booklet was sufficiently brisk that a second printing took place in 1955.

1954

LIN   Linotype Model Fleet 54 introduced by Linotype & Machinery Ltd. It was a machine designed principally for TTS tape operation at 10 to 12 lines per minute.

SO   Ludlow Typograph Co. introduced the Brightype conversion system, a method requiring a letterpress forme to be sprayed with a black lacquer and the printing surface wiped clean with a rubber pad and made reflective. Afterwards the treated forme was photographed on a Brightype camera to yield a photomechanical master.

TYP   Annual Award for Newspaper Design inaugurated in Britain by the magazine *Printing World.*

TYP   Glasgow Herald became the first user of the Jubilee typeface (see 1947) from Linotype.

TYP   Minerva typeface designed for Linotype composition by Reynolds Stone, the outstandingly gifted wood-engraver (see 1979).

PTS   Early use of the term *filmsetting* occurred in *Printing Review.*

PTS   Higonnet-Moyroud phototypesetting machine entered field trial as the Photon 100 at the *Patriot Ledger* newspaper in Quincy, Massachusetts. George Prescott Lowe was the pioneering proprietor.

PTS   Second major work produced on the Higonnet-Moyroud phototypesetting system, namely *The New Testament in Cadenced Form* designed by Morton C. Bradley, Jr.

PTS   Leadless type supplement produced under the direction of H. O. Smith for the magazine *Print In Britain.* Included among the pages were specimen settings by the Intertype Fotosetter, Rotofoto, Monophoto, and Photon systems with displayed areas by the Hadego machine.

CAT   Georges Bafour of the Imprimerie Nationale, Andre Blanchard, and Francois Raymond framed a patent application in France which constituted one of the earliest proposals for a computer-controlled composition system. It envisaged the use of a digital computer for text processing and became known succinctly as the BBR patent.

CAT   Magnetic core memory patent of Dr. An Wang sold to IBM. It was a technology applied in countless digital computers.

OCR   First commercial optical scanner installed by the Intelligent Machine Corporation. It was used for reading numeric information on credit card slips.

1955

LIN   Simplified Arabic script developed for composition on Linotype machines. Essentially the scheme involved the deployment of two forms of a character, instead of the usual four.

TO   London Society of Compositors merged with the Printing Machine Managers' Trade Society to form the London Typographical Society.

TF   John S. Thompson, inventor of the Thompson Typecaster, died on 8 July.

TYP   Christian H. Kleukens died. He set up and ran a press in Mainz and designed several typefaces, such as: Kleukens Antiqua (Bauer 1900), Helga (Stempel 1912), Ratio Roman (Stempel 1923), Omega (Stempel 1926), and Scriptura (Stempel 1926).

TYP   John Dreyfus appointed typographic adviser to the Monotype Corporation Ltd. on the retirement of Stanley Morison. In 1958 the decision of Monotype to embrace the Univers type family was on the recommendation of the new adviser. John Dreyfus has written with distinction on typographic subjects. His books (often in limited edition) include: *The Survival of Baskerville's Punches* (1949), *The Work of Jan Van Krimpen* (1952), *Italic Quartet* (1966), and *The History of the Nonesuch Press* (1981).

PTS   *The Geneva Bible,* an essay by Stanley Morison, was produced as a booklet at the London School of Printing using the Rotofoto system for composition. Impetus for the booklet was a visit by Stanley Morison to the LSP to inspect the Rotofoto installation. He was accompanied by George Westover. Seemingly the two men were good friends, in spite of the alienation of George Westover from the Monotype Corporation Ltd.

PTS   Another milestone publication composed on the Rotofoto system at the London School of Printing appeared under the title of *Behind the Magnesium Curtain* by George Westover. To underline the universal application of phototypeset material to photomechanically prepared printing surfaces, the booklet was issued in two editions produced respectively by letterpress from the then novel powderless- etched plates and by offset-lithography.

PTS   Linofilm photocomposing system previewed at IPEX. Intelligence of the system lodged in the ample keyboard which yielded a 15-level punched paper control tape. Precise justification data was injected into the tape as a product of the electronic logic. Housed in the photo-unit were 18 matrix grids with 88 characters apiece. Image exposures were formed from a stationary grid, a binary shutter determining character selection. Type size was established by a zoom lens system. Laydown of characters in a text line was accomplished by a traversing carriage of optical elements (see 1959).

abcdefghijklmnopqrst
ABCDEFGHIJKLMNOP
1234567890 .,;:'"«»&!?
Univers

1956

TF   Death occurred of Charles Malin, the Parisian punchcutter. He prepared punches for Perpetua by Eric Gill, for Dante by Giovanni Mardersteig, and for a recutting of Arrighi by Frederic Warde.

TF   Klingspor typefoundry closed in Offenbach am Main.

SO   Addressograph-Multigraph Corporation purchased rights to the Varityper machine and created a specialised composition division bearing the name (see 1913).

TYP   Letraset adapted, for a method of composing headlines, the simple principle of the water slide transfer.

TYP   W. A. Dwiggins, the remarkable American designer, died. His achievements included the creation of a number of type families for the Mergenthaler Linotype Co. exemplified by Metro (1929), Caledonia (1938), Eldorado (1951), and Falcon (1961).

TYP   Max Miedinger designed the Neue Haas-Grotesk typeface for the Haas foundry. Stempel AG negotiated rights to the design in 1960 and on release re-named it Helvetica. In 1961 the family was adapted for Linotype hot-metal equipment and later for phototypesetting. Helvetica has been one of the most successful sanserif designs of the post-war era.

PTS   First Intertype Fotosetter installed in the United Kingdom by the Printing Department of the Corporation of Glasgow.

PTS   Phototypesetting developments of Higonnet and Moyroud reached the production stage with the Photon 200 machine, a direct-entry device consisting of a keyboard with a typewritten record, a control

abcdefghijklmnopqrstu
ABCDEFGHIJKLMN
XYZ 1234567890 12345
Caledonia

unit, and a photo-unit. Many prime inventions were involved, such as the selection and stroboscopic imaging of characters from a spinning photo-matrix disc and the use of a stepping optical escapement carriage for the spacing of characters. Stored on the photo-matrix disc were 16 type styles that could be imaged in a dozen point sizes through a turret of lenses. Numerous composition functions were embedded in the logic. It was a universal system capable of virtually any kind of work: a complete composing room as the promoters of the day pronounced.

PTS Field trial of the Linofilm phototypesetting system commenced at the *Daily News* of New York to be followed by an additional test site in 1957 at the commercial typesetting house of H. O. Bullard in the same city.

1957

LIN Hydraquadder attachment released for use on British-made Linotype machines. As the name implied, the vice jaws were moved hydraulically.

LIN Intertype Corporation and Harris-Seybold merged to form the Harris-Intertype Corporation.

SO Varityper Division of the Addressograph-Multigraph Corporation disclosed the Fotolist System: a sequential card camera that photographed typewritten records. It provided a new and rational approach to the sorting and composition of directories, parts lists, and other publications of listings (see 1960).

TYP Constitution of E13B founts and the design of symbols for magnetic ink character recognition (MICR) agreed jointly by the Office Equipment Manufacturers' Association and the American Bankers' Association.

TYP Death occurred of Bruce Rogers, the eminent American typographer. His creations embraced the typeface Centaur which surfaced intially as a titling fount for the Metropolitan Museum of New York in 1915. Later the design was adapted, and extended with a lower-case alphabet, for Monotype machines in 1929. To accompany the roman, Frederic Warde developed an italic known variously as Arrighi and Centaur. Bruce Rogers has many other typographic credits, not least the Lectern Bible completed at the Oxford University Press in 1935.

TYP Association Typographique Internationale (A.Typ.I.) inaugurated. It serves as a focal point for typographic interests and is dedicated to securing copyright protection for original type designs.

TO Wynkyn de Worde Society constituted on 12 September. It is a luncheon club that meets bi-monthly at Stationers' Hall in London and has a broad membership interested in all aspects of fine printing.

PTS Early use of the term *photosetting* occurred in *Americana Annual*.

PTS One of the earliest phototypeset books to be produced in the United Kingdom appeared, namely *Private Angelo* by Eric Linklater published privately as a Christmas gift by Sir Allen and Richard Lane. It was set on the Intertype Fotosetter in Garamond and printed by offset-lithography at McCorquodale & Co. Ltd. Commercial issue by Penguin Books followed in March 1958.

PTS Rotofoto project, masterminded by George Westover, was brought to an end.

PTS Last of the series of booklets produced on the Rotofoto system at the London School of Printing under the title *Modern and Historical Typography* by Imre Reiner was issued.

PTS Individual and interchangeable photo-matrices were developed for the Monophoto Filmsetter to replace the solid glass plate or grid previously supplied. It was a development that signalled initial commercial acceptance of the machine.

PTS First Monophoto Filmsetter installed in the United Kingdom by Photoprint Plates Ltd. of Basildon, Essex.

ABCDEFGHIJKL
abcdefghijklmnop

Centaur

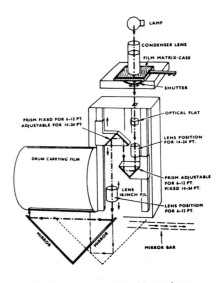

Optical system of the Monophoto filmsetter

1958

LIN   Linotype & Machinery Ltd. ceased to manufacture spare parts for the Linotype Model 1 (see 1890 and 1892).

LIN   Intertype Monarch keyboardless linecaster introduced for teletypesetter tape operation.

LIN   Assets of the Teletypesetter Corporation acquired by Fairchild Graphic Equipment.

TYP   Jan van Krimpen died on 28 October (see 1892).

TYP   Adrian Frutiger appointed art director of the Deberny & Peignot typefoundry. His type-design work has been distinguished, plentiful, and consonant with modern technology. Attributable typefaces include: Phoebus (1953), Ondine (1954), Egyptienne (1956), Meridien (1956), Univers (1957), Apollo (1962), Serifa (1967), OCR-B (1968), Iridium (1975), Frutiger (1976), Icone (1980), Breughel (1982), Versailles (1982), and Centennial (1986). Frutiger is currently (1986) typographic consultant to the Linotype Group.

PTS   Centenary year of H. Berthold AG which marked the entry of the company into photolettering with the Diatype machine. Over 10,000 of the units have been installed commercially.

PTS   Photon Inc. confronted the problems of correcting phototypeset material with the introduction of the discretionary hyphen and tape-merging system. Uncounted text on punched paper tape was initially produced on typewriter-based keyboards with discretionary hyphens inserted as necessary. Using the typescript as a proof, a second tape containing corrections was prepared, together with codes identifying their locations. Afterwards the two tapes were merged into a third for controlling a specially-modified Photon 200 phototypesetter.

PTS   One of the most notable works among phototypeset incunabula was published by Funk & Wagnalls, the *Standard International Dictionary* consisting of over 1,500 pages in a couple of volumes. Composition was completed in Boston on a battery of Photon 200 machines: the latest incarnation of research by Rene Higonnet and Louis Moyroud.

PTS   Four books, set on the Linofilm (see 1955), were published in the USA. They were: *The Story of Holly and Ivy* by Rumer Godden (Viking Press); *Skipping Island* by Emma I. Brock (Alfred A. Knopf); *Satellite of the Sun* by Athelstan F. Spilhaus (Viking Press); and *Elihu the Musical Gnu* by Hannah Simons (The Platt & Munk Co. Inc.).

PTS   ATF Typesetter surfaced from roots in strike-on composition as manifest by compatibility with the Justowriter system. Two units comprised the ATF Typesetter, a Recorder in the form of a typewriter keyboard complete with hard copy and paper tape punch and a Reproducer photo-unit activated by a control tape. Image exposures occurred from an oscillating photo-matrix disc and movement of the film secured character escapement.

PTS   Demarcation agreement reached in the United Kingdom between the typographic and lithographic trades unions for the handling of phototypeset material. It amounted to a ludicrous accord as far as running an efficient business was concerned. In essence the typographic unions assembled textual material leaving space for pictorial subjects to be inserted separately by lithographic personnel.

1959

LIN   Linotype & Machinery Ltd. disclosed the Linotype Model 70 series of linecasting machines. Five models were included in the range: the Model 70 (superseded the Model 50), the Model 72 (superseded the Super-Range), the Model 73 (superseded the Model 53), the Model 78 (superseded the Model 48), and the Model 79 for TTS tape operation at 12 lines a minute. Casting speeds were variable between 7 to 12 lines a minute.

abcdefghijklmnopqrst
ABCDEFGHIJKLMNOP
1234567890 .,;:''«»&!?

Frutiger

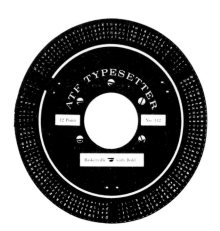

Photo-matrix disc of the ATF Typesetter

TYP   Letraset Ltd. formed to exploit commercially the idea of transfer lettering (see 1956 and 1961).

PTS   Visual Graphics Corporation established.

PTS   First composition to be done on the ATF Typesetter in Europe appeared in the external house magazine *Partners in Progress* from Pershke Price.

PTS   In the month of May the first production models of the Linofilm system emerged from the factory at Wellsboro in Pennsylvania.

PTS   First production model of the Linofilm delivered to the *National Geographic* magazine in August.

PTS   Intertype Corporation sued Photon Inc. for alleged infringement of two phototypesetting patents in the name of the inventor Tansel. After a series of appeals up to the level of the Supreme Court of the United States, the original judgement deeming the patents to be old and invalid was upheld in 1964.

PTS   Higonnet and Moyroud had notions leading to development of the Photon ZIP: the fastest second-generation phototypesetter ever produced running at 1,000,000 to 2,000,000 ens an hour. Characters were stored, with a xenon lamp behind each, as stationary photo-matrix grids. Placement of characters in a text line was determined by a continuously-moving lens allied to flash timing. Base alignment derived from bouncing images through a tunnel of mirrors to settle at the appropriate level. Patents were granted in 1960 (see 1964).

1960

LIN   Tape-allotting system developed to optimise the productivity of teletypesetting plants.

PTS   Compugraphic Corporation founded by Bill Garth (a former President of Photon Inc.) and Ellis Hanson. It initially developed, manufactured, and marketed special-purpose hard-wired computers for typesetting control and graduated in 1968 to the provision of inexpensive phototypesetting machines. Success of the company stemmed from the realisation that the printing industry comprised overwhelmingly small-scale commercial enterprises requiring budget-priced equipment in the modern idiom. By the 1970s the company had become a leader in many market sectors.

SO   Early use of the term *cold-type composition* occurred in *The Times Literary Supplement*.

SO   First British commercial installation made of a Fotolist system: a sequential card camera that photographed typewritten records. It was used to produce the *British National Bibliography* from January 1961 and for the next ten years. Production proceeded at a rate of two cards per second. The cards were stopped for imaging under continuous light through a mechanical shutter. Manufacturer of the system was the Varityper Division of Addressograph-Multigraph.

PTS   Phototypositor display photolettering machine launched by the Visual Graphics Corporation. More than 7,000 units had been sold by 1979.

PTS   First Alphatype phototypesetting machine inaugurated. It was noted for the high quality of typographic output obtained from photo-matrix grids that remained stationary on exposure, a different master fount being deployed for every image size.

PTS   CAPS Ltd. developed the Graphatron: a phototypesetting machine that exposed characters on to a reel of Kalfax material which revealed the latent image on application of heat. Once assembled, the text was justified by optical projection and anamorphic adjustment from the Kalfax reel on to a second photo-sensitive surface. The project did not reach the production stage.

PTS   Theodore H. Maiman (born 1927) first generated a laser beam at the Hughes Laboratory in Malibu. It was not until 1972 that the laser first cropped up in phototypesetting as a substitute for the xenon flash tube in a Photon 560 machine.

1961

TYP   Instant lettering by the dry transfer method introduced by Letraset (see 1956).

SO   IBM Selectric Typewriter introduced, the first to employ a golf-ball typing head. The principle was destined to have a major influence and upheaval on direct-impression composing methods.

SO   Taunton Telephone Directory composed on the Listomatic sequential card camera system and reproduced as powderless-etched plates for letterpress printing. It was the first public telephone directory to be produced in Britain by this method.

PTS   Crosfield Electronics Ltd. appointed as a manufacturing agent for Photon Inc. in the United Kingdom and many other territories. Direct result of the deal was development of the Photon 540 system (see 1962).

CAT   Michael Barnett headed a group at the Massachusetts Institute of Technology that successfully programmed a digital computer to drive a phototypesetting machine, namely the Photon 200.

CAT   Compugraphic Corporation promoted its first product, the Directory Tape Processor: a special-purpose computer for composition.

1962

LIN   DRUPA saw the European debut of the Linotype Elektron. Publicised as the fastest linecaster in the world, a speed of 15 newspaper lines per minute was pronounced. Many engineering refinements were featured, such as continuous assembly and straight-line delivery of matrices for casting.

SO   Scotchprint, a translucent proofing and conversion film, announced by 3M. It was a stable plastic material with an ink-receptive surface used for reproducing letterpress formes on standard proofing presses. Output was equivalent to a photographic positive.

LIN   Universal Perforator revealed for teletypesetting: the new keyboard could reckon with unit and non-unit cut matrices.

TYP   Death occurred of S. H. de Roos, the Dutch book and type designer. His typefaces included Hollandsche Mediaeval (1912), Zilver Type (1915), Erasmus Mediaeval (1923), Egmont (1933), Libra (1938), Simplex (1939), and De Roos (1947). Most of the alphabets were created for the Amsterdam Typefoundry and additionally rendered as Intertype matrices, while a couple of the designs served private presses.

PTS   Intertype Fotomatic introduced, a tape-driven version of the forerunning Fotosetter. Teletypesetter tape and keyboards applied. The fotomats on this machine contained a pair of characters and not just one as on the Fotosetter.

PTS   Crosfield Electronics Ltd. launched the Photon 540 System. It was essentially an outgrowth of the preceding Photon 200 equipment and functioned on the same basic principles, but separated the text keyboarding and text exposure processes. Paper tape served as the interface between the two stages, whereas the Photon 200 integrated them as a direct-entry keyboard-driven machine. Machines related to the Photon 540 surfacing at the same time were the Photon 513 and 560.

PTS   First British book set on the Linofilm system produced by William Clowes & Sons Ltd. Bodley Head published the edition, a biography of Scott Fitzgerald by Andrew Turnbull.

PTS   Alphanumeric Inc. formed as an electronic typesetting service. It additionally developed the Alphanumeric Photocomposer System, the APS-2 based on digital CRT techniques (see 1967).

CAT   Research project into computer-controlled typesetting commenced under the direction of John Duncan of the University of Newcastle-upon-Tyne.

CAT   Perry Publications Inc. of West Palm Beach (see 1965) inaugurated an

RCA 301 computer configuration embracing an 88Mb. magnetic disc and utilising a 50,000-word exception dictionary supported by hyphenation logic to process TTS linecaster control tapes.

CAT   *Los Angeles Times* commissioned an RCA 301 computer system for generating TTS linecasting tapes.

1963

MON   Unit-shift attachment appeared for Monotype casters and for Monophoto filmsetters. It offered larger matrix cases of 16 x 17 rows providing 272 characters overall, the ability to intermix in a single row characters of two different unit values, and a bigger keyboard layout of 14 x 12 rows of buttons as opposed to 14 x 11 formerly.

MON   Varigear attachment perfected for Monotype composition casters. Greater convenience of control over running speeds was afforded.

TYP   Initial Teaching Alphabet inaugurated by Sir James Pitman.

TYP   Matthew Carter appointed type designer by Crosfield Electronics Ltd. He eventually moved on to join the Linotype Group of Companies and contributed handsomely to their typographical accomplishments. In 1981 Matthew Carter, together with Mike Parker, became a principal of the fledgeling Bitstream Inc., a manufacturer and supplier of digital founts. Type designs attributable to him embrace Auriga (1970), Olympian (1970), CRT Gothic (1974), Video (1977), and Galliard (1978).

PTS   Monotype Photolettering Machine inaugurated. It was a manually-operated device with characters selected for exposure by dialling at the front of the unit. Prime application was for displayed composition, though the original development stimulus arose from cartographic demands.

CAT   Early use of the terms *computer-aided* and *computer-controlled typesetting* occurred.

CAT   Compugraphic Corporation released the Linasec special-purpose typesetting computer. Conceptually the Linasec was straightforward. It required that unjustified text tapes be fed to the machine which accumulated the character widths and added end-of-line codes to an output TTS tape for the operation of linecasters and TTS-compatible phototypesetters. No hyphenation logic was provided, instead a fall-off word was displayed electronically for the human operator to pick an apt break point. Fabrication of the Linasec was in hard-wired logic.

TO   National Graphical Association formed by amalgamation of the Typographical Association and the London Typographical Society.

CAT   Rocappi Inc. established as an electronic typesetting service bureau founded on the RCA 301 computer. Shortly afterwards a British affiliate was formed as Rocappi Ltd. One of the first works processed by the latter organisation was the *Collected Poems 1934-1952* of Dylan Thomas published by J. M. Dent Ltd. as part of Everyman's Library in 1966.

1964

LIN   Intertype Monarch linecaster with an integral keyboard announced (see 1958).

TO   London Typographical Society merged with the Typographical Association to form the National Graphical Association.

SO   Converkal conversion system announced by Kal/Graphic Inc., the system demanded the pre-heating of a letterpress forme and its impression on to coated heat-sensitive film via a conventional reproduction proofing press. Ouput was the equivalent of a film negative, the heat and pressure clearing the image areas.

SO   IBM released the Magnetic Tape Selectric Typewriter (MTST), a strike-on system of composition which stored keystrokes (or data) on 16mm. magnetic cartridge tape sprocketed on one side and able to

abcdefghijklmnopqrst
ABCDEFGHIJKLMNO
1234567890 .,;:'«»&!?
Auriga

abcdefghijklmnopqrs
ABCDEFGHIJKLMN
XYZ 1234567890 .,;:"
Olympian

hold 8,400 characters over a length of 35 feet. Longer tapes were provided.

SO Word processing coined as a new technical term in the English language by IBM. It was presaged by the German expression *Textverarbeitung.*

TYP Colin Brignall joined the type-design studio of Letraset and later became head of the department. His more enduring typefaces encompass Aachen Bold (1969), Revue (1969), and Romic (1979).

P&J *CIS Newsletter,* a fortnightly publication devoted to new typesetting technologies, was inaugurated by Arthur E. Gardner. It was discontinued in the early 1970s. CIS stood for Composition Information Services.

PTS H. Berthold AG acquired Filmklischee GmbH and the Starsettograph headlining machine which eventually spawned the Staromat and Superstar devices.

PTS First Photon ZIP (see 1959) phototypesetter installed at the National Library of Medicine in Bethesda near Washington. It accepted formatted text as computer-generated magnetic tape. Subject of the installation was *Index Medicus,* a monthly publication of 700 pages containing medical abstracts. As an early example of database composition, the phenomenal speed of the Photon ZIP was apposite.

CAT Computaprint Ltd. established in London. It used a Photon ZIP phototypesetter for output and constituted an early example of an electronic typesetting service for custodians of computer databases that needed publishing.

PTS Linofilm Quick unveiled. Two photo-matrix grids were contained in the machine. Each carried 184 characters, a number equivalent to a linecaster magazine in upper- and lower-rail. Point sizes equated to the photo-matrices, as optical enlargement and reduction was precluded by the system. Exposures were prompted by illumination of an entire stationary grid with a complex of optical wedges selecting a character and deflecting its image to a common optical path. Most important was data compatibility with justified TTS tapes. Speed was 14 characters per second. Character widths were stored on hardware plugs.

PTS Fototronic 480 system announced by the Intertype Co. Like the contemporaneous Linofilm and Photon 540 equipment, the intelligence of the Fototronic 480 resided in the keyboard which created an 8-level control tape. Two photo-matrix discs were accommodated in the exposure unit. Character widths were stored optically on the discs and the information sensed in parallel. Selection and imaging of characters from the continuously spinning discs was by direct access optical codes and by stroboscopic flash.

J&P John Duncan contributed a review of computerised composition entitled *Look! No Hands!* to *The Penrose Annual.* It stimulated a great deal of debate on the portents for the new technology and served to galvanise action in some quarters.

CAT Trials to produce *Astronomical Ephemeris* directly from the data on punched cards of the Nautical Almanac Office were successfully completed by the HMSO. The Monophoto filmsetter served as the output device.

CAT Richard Clay Ltd. became the first British firm to install a computer as an aid to typesetting, namely the Linasec (see 1963).

CAT *Miami Herald* harnessed an IBM 1620 computer system for linecaster control and updated the installation to an IBM 360/30 in 1967.

1965

LIN Matrotype Ltd., a manufacturer of hot-metal matrices, founded. It was the first to produce the popular Univers typeface for linecasting machines.

PTS Monophoto Filmsetter Mark 3 revealed. It incorporated a simplified

abcdefghijklmnopqrstuv
ABCDEFGHIJKLMNOPQ
1234567890 .,;:''«»&

Romic

Photo-matrix disc for Fototronic 480

gearbox, an increase in running speed, and a method of proportional justification for text lines.

CAT Monotype Paper Tape Conversion Unit revealed, a system that accepted input as narrow computer-generated punched paper tapes, translated the codes, and output 31-channel spools for controlling Monotype and Monophoto machines. The device established compatibility between digital computers and Monotype products.

PTS Photon 550 phototypesetting system was shown at the TPG exhibition in Paris. It had much in common with the Photon 540 (see 1962), but could be operated directly from a keyboard or alternatively run from uncounted punched paper tape with hyphenation points determined by a human monitor.

TO Association of Correctors of the Press was integrated into the National Graphical Association.

PTS Model of Linofilm Quick announced accommodating four photo-matrix grids (see 1964). It was essentially a text setting machine as its forerunner.

PTS Photon 713-10 introduced, a phototypesetter fashioned from discrete component solid-state electronics (as the contemporary Linofilm Quick) and offering an automatic mix of 8 type styles in 8 type sizes or 64 typographical variations under tape control. Many novel optical aspects were embodied in the system, such as extended escapement carriage steps to accommodate several character exposures placed side by side through differential flash timings. Such rationalisation of mechanical movement enabled speeds of 20 characters per second to be obtained.

PTS Mergenthaler Linotype Co. and CBS Laboratories embarked on development of the Linotron 1010, an early essay into cathode ray tube (CRT) typesetting. In essence the Linotron 1010 operated from fully-formatted magnetic tape; ran at speeds of up to 1,090 characters per second; encompassed four photo-matrix grids each with 256 characters; selected characters in a manner similar to an image dissector; and wrote out an entire page on the face of the output CRT for projection to the sensitive plane by way of a 2:1 reduction lens.

PTS Dr.-Ing. Rudolf Hell announced the Digiset phototypesetter, the first to utilise digitised founts for image generation on an output cathode ray tube (CRT) from whence exposures on to photo-sensitive materials were made. RCA in the United States of America announced a version of the same machine known as the Videocomp.

CAT Digital Equipment Corporation announced the PDP-8 minicomputer which became the processing unit for many early electronic typesetting systems.

CAT Thomson Computerset System installed at the *Evening Post* in Reading. It was originally based on an Elliott 803 computer and later on a Model 903. Control tapes for a Photon 713 phototypesetter were generated by the system. Multiplexors were used to connect a dozen input keyboards on-line to the computer and a dozen paper tape punches. Development work was conducted jointly by Elliott Automation Ltd. and by the Thomson Organisation. Dr. Tom Margerison was a consultant to the project.

CAT IBM 360 computer revealed. It was programmed for typesetting by various software contractors and by the hardware manufacturer, but tended to make a somewhat expensive composition system and was overshadowed in the printing industry by the cheaper IBM 1130 machine.

CAT Typesetting system promoted by IBM based on the 1130 computer. It was a straightforward operation involving the input of uncounted punched paper tapes which the computer accepted and injected into the text stream end-of-line codes (including hyphenated breaks), and output justified punched paper tapes for the control of linecasters and various phototypesetters.

CAT International Computers Ltd. developed generalised batch process

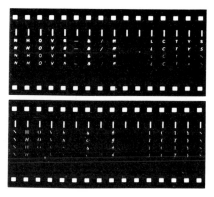

Photo-matrix film strips for the Photon 713-10

composition software to run on its 1900 series of computers. Output comprised 6-level TTS tapes for linecaster control and 8-channel tapes for conversion to 31-channel Monotype and Monophoto spools.

CAT   The Monotype Corporation Ltd. brought to the United Kingdom the Swiss-engineered GSA Computer Typesetting System: the initials stood for Guttinger Satz Automation. Various elements were encompassed by the system, such as a non-justifying typewriter-based keyboard, a tape-merging correction station, an automatic hyphenating unit, a computer generating TTS control tapes, and a Monotron computer creating 31-channel output tapes for Monotype casters and for Monophoto machines.

OCR   Perry Publications of West Palm Beach in Florida spent something in the region of $700,000 on an Electronic Retina Computing Reader produced by Recognition Equipment Inc. The installation was employed for reading typescripts in a newspaper production office: the earliest application of OCR techniques in the printing industry (see 1962).

1966

MC   SAM hot-metal system developed by M. H. Whittaker & Sons Ltd.: the initials stood for Sets All Matrices. In production, the matrices were assembled by hand in special sticks for insertion into the casting unit which yielded slugs. Ludlow, Linotype, Intertype, and Nebitype matrices could be used.

MON   Varigear refinement supplied for Monotype Super Caster (see 1963).

SO   IBM announced the Magnetic Tape Selectric Composer (MTSC). It was a strike-on method of composition offering proportionally-spaced characters with some comparability to printers' typefaces. Data tapes were compatible with the MTST system (see 1964).

SO   Varityper 720 strike-on composition system disclosed as a replacement for the forerunning Model 660. Improvements in the new model related primarily to aids for increased productivity.

TYP   Paul Bennett died on 18 December. He had for many years acted as the leader and spur of The Typophiles in New York (see 1933) editing many of their endearing keepsakes. His daily work was deeply involved with the typographical activities and developments of the Mergenthaler Linotype Co. Joseph Blumenthal, in his autobiography, described Paul Bennett as 'the typographic conscience of our generation'.

PTS   Production speed of the Linofilm photo-unit increased from 12.5 to 18 characters per second (see 1955).

PTS   Photon 713-20 phototypesetter emerged. Fundamentally the machine worked in the same way as the preceding Photon 713-10 (see 1965), but embodied extra hard-wired logic permitting the acceptance of *unjustified* input tapes. On receipt of the endless string of text, the logic effected line breaks and justification automatically prior to exposure, but could not achieve the elegance of hyphenation. It was a milestone development that gave rise to the 'intelligent' phototypesetter.

PTS   Kodak introduced a range of stabilisation papers for phototypesetting. Incorporated in the photo-sensitive emulsion were the developing agents which remained dormant until activated by chemical processing. With appropriate input/output cassette systems developed by the phototypesetting machinery manufacturers, the materials could be processed in daylight with desk-top Ektamatic units. Darkroom loading of the paper was necessary. Images tended to be fugitive unless kept properly and refrigerated storage of the unexposed rolls was recommended. Grade S papers were furnished for strobe flash machines and Grade T papers for tungsten exposures (see 1972).

PTS   Photon Inc. initiated action against the Mergenthaler Linotype Co. for the infringement of several patents relating to character escapement and to storage of character widths. It took years for the appeal process to be exhausted when in 1970 an out-of-court settlement was reached requiring the Mergenthaler Linotype Co. to pay Photon Inc. some $2.5 millions.

CAT Compugraphic Corporation expanded its range of special-purpose typesetting computers with announcement of the Justape which sold for a little over $8,200 as opposed to the $15,000 to $18,000 for the Linasec (see 1963). In principle, the Justape operated in a manner similar to the Linasec and performed identical functions, but the electronic display to permit monitored hyphenation was removed from the standard machine configuration and became an option.

CAT Digital Equipment Corporation instituted composition software for the PDP-8 computer. In essence the system accepted unjustified input tapes, used the software program to determine the ends of lines and to hyphenate straddle words, and output the results as justified punched paper tapes. Hence the system was conceived as a *batch operation* whereby the entire job was processed serially from beginning to end. The earliest PDP-8 systems had recourse to a 4K, 12-bit memory sufficient to hold justification and hyphenation logic, the latter supported by an exception dictionary of 250 words.

KEY Purdy and McIntosh developed keyboards with exchangeable button banks which allowed a typewriter-based or a linecaster layout to be employed alternately within the same framework. Other vanguard facilities included the generation of multiple codes by electronic logic from a single keystroke, and a modular approach to construction was adopted as instanced by a host non-counting keyboard being converted to a counting keyboard by plugging in a justification calculator.

1967

LIN Linotype & Machinery Ltd. ceased the manufacture of spare parts for the venerable Linotype Models 4, 4SM, 6, and 6SM (see 1911, 1922, 1923, and 1926).

LIN Single-magazine version of the Linotype Elektron linecaster released. It was labelled the Elektron Meteor.

MON Fairchild TTS System 440 developed which permitted automatic access to side magazines when operating a linecaster from tape.

MON After 60 years of pre-eminence, the Monotype Model D Keyboard was joined by an alternative, namely the Monotype Electronic Perforator. Automatic line justification was the benefit bestowed by the newcomer which resulted in considerable boosts to production, particularly on tabulated settings.

TYP Stanley Morison died on 11 October.

J&P Appearance of the first issue of *The Journal of Typographic Research* edited by Merald E. Wrolstad. Its title was changed in 1971 to *Visible Language*.

SO Early use of the term *strike-on composition* occurred in *Offset Processes*.

PTS Varityper announced the Headliner 810: a photolettering device utilising a plastic photo-matrix disc, relying on the selection of characters by manual dialling, and practising contact exposures to obtain superb quality images.

PTS Monophoto Filmsetter Mark 4 uncovered. Several improvements were embodied, principally the enlargement of the photo-matrix case from 272 to 340 characters and spaces.

PTS Linotron 1010 (see 1965) installed at the US Government Printing Office.

PTS Linofilm COL-28 model launched: the COL stood for Computer Only Linofilm and the figure signified an enlarged carousel of 28 photo-matrix grids. Acceptance of 6-level data tapes established some degree of compatibility with computers, instead of the earlier idiosyncratic 15-level variety (see 1955 and 1966).

PTS First British installation of the Linofilm Quick system completed at the Essex Chronicle Series Ltd. in Chelmsford.

PTS Photon 713-5 phototypesetter announced at DRUPA. It was manufactured from integrated circuits and offered a typographic dress of 4 type styles and 2 point sizes: a curtailed specification compared to the bigger Photon 713-10 which permitted a keen price (see 1965).

PTS Varityper Division of Addressograph-Multigraph (now AM International) entered the phototypesetting machinery market with the model AM 725 obtained under licence from Photon Inc. Text was input as justified TTS-style paper tape for exposure at a rate of 12 characters per second. The optical system disclosed lateral movement of the photo-matrix disc and lamp assembly for character escapement; a variation in the length of the light path and lens position therein for type sizing; and stroboscopic imaging for character selection.

PTS Fairchild Graphic Equipment entered the phototypesetting machinery market at DRUPA with the models PTS 2000 and PTS 8000: the initials stood for PhotoTextSetter. Both machines were compatible with the teletypesetter keyboards and punched tape equipment by the same manufacturer. Many novel features were contained in the two units, such as character escapement by a rotating mirror on the PTS 2000 and fount-sequential composition on the PTS 8000.

PTS Having established a strong market position in photolettering, H. Berthold AG diversified into keyboard-operated phototypesetting with release of the Diatronic machine at DRUPA. It was a direct-entry device. Operator feedback comprised a display of the last character tapped and a ribbon scale denoting the current condition of the text line. Character escapement was by an oscillating mirror deflecting images on to a curved sensitive plane. Fount storage was on eight photo-matrix grids which remained stationary when in the exposure position. Selection of characters involved mechanical shuttering, movement of prisms, and singling out a flash tube for activation from a multiple bank.

PTS PM Filmsetter 1001 exhibited at DRUPA: the initials represented the names of the inventors Peter Purdy and Ronald McIntosh whose efforts were supported by K. S. Paul Ltd. It proved to be the first popular CRT machine after transmogrification into the Linotron 505 during the same year when K. S. Paul Ltd. was merged to become Linotype-Paul Ltd. Characters were stored on photo-matrix grids and subjected to a flying spot scan. Afterwards the rasterised characters were received by a bank of photomultipliers. One was energised to select the wanted character. To complete the process, the photomultiplier output was utilised to create a succession of consecutive and single scan lines on the print-out CRT. Imaging of the scan lines on to the sensitive paper or film was through a reduction lens. Juxtaposition of scan lines on the output material was accomplished by continuous movement of the lens along a carriage which served to assemble the text at a resolution of 650 or 1,300 lines per inch. Speeds in the region of 120 newspaper lines per minute were quoted. Controller logic was hard wired.

PTS First Digiset machine was installed at Lux Bildstudio GmbH at Neu-Isenburg near Frankfurt.

PTS Alphanumeric Inc. launched the APS-2 phototypesetter, a CRT machine making use of digital founts stored as run-length coding. That is the start/stop points of the vertical strokes employed to synthesise character shapes on the output CRT were described and stored in computer memory. Compression of the fount data was practised to occupy computer memory as frugally as possible.

PTS IBM joined the growing interest in cathode ray tube phototypesetting by divulging the IBM 2680 machine, a specially-packaged version of the concurrent APS-3 by Alphanumeric Inc. and designed to run as a peripheral of the IBM 360 mainframe computer.

PTS A. B. Dick Co. announced the Videojet 960 non-impact printer.

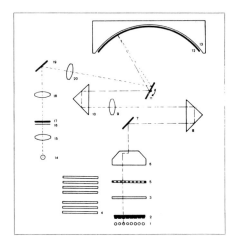

Diatronic optical system

Diatronic photo-matrix grid

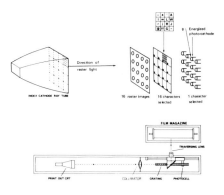

Schematic of Linotron 505 phototypesetter

CAT   Muset special-purpose typesetting computer released by the inventor Hunter Geddes. It was designed to produce TTS control tapes. Word divisions relied upon the keyboard operator embedding discretionary hyphens in the input data tapes. Marketing of the machine devolved to Muirhead & Co. Ltd.

CAT   Penta Systems founded to automate composition internally at Typesetters Inc., the principal shareholder and initiator of the scheme being the owner of the latter company.

CAT   Composition Systems Inc. established as a software house developing typesetting programs to run on hardware by the Digital Equipment Corporation. Initially PDP-8 computers were used, followed by PDP-11 and VAX machines (see 1986).

CAT   Comprite Ltd. established as a composition software house in the United Kingdom with Alan Hughes at the helm. Its initial systems were founded on the programs of CSI (see above), but as time elapsed divergence between the two increased.

1968

SO   Varityper 1010 strike-on system divulged. It was characterised by a powered keyboard with the response of an electric typewriter.

TYP   Leslie Usherwood founded Typesettra at Toronto as a trade headline and photocomposition service. It diversified as a type design studio in 1977. Several typefaces are attributable to Typesettra and in particular to Leslie Usherwood, namely Caxton, Flange, Graphis Bold, and Lynton. Most phototypesetting machinery manufacturers have licensed designs from Typesettra.

J&P   *Computer Peripherals and Typesetting*, a book by Arthur Phillips, was published; the first authoritative account and description of developments in the field of automated composition.

LIN   Ludlow Typograph Co. absorbed by International Metals and Machines Inc. It continued to function as a division in the new group.

PTS   Linofilm Super Quick released. It ran faster at 40 characters per second than the earlier Linofilm Quick and extended the type size range to an upper limit of 72 points by interposing a pair of lenses into the optical path magnifying the master characters respectively two- and four-fold (see 1964 and 1965).

PTS   Intertype Co. launched the Fototronic 1200 system housing 5 photo-matrix discs mounted around a ferris-wheel mechanism. It was engineered in integrated electronic circuits, instead of the fragile technology of the preceding Fototronic 480 with a pair of photo-matrix discs (see 1964). Type sizing was by a zoom lens system and character escapement emanated from lateral movement of the sensitive plane allied to a fine optical adjustment. First British installation was at Yorkshire Post Newspapers.

PTS   Fototronic CRT, employing digital founts, introduced by the Intertype Co.

PTS   Compugraphic Corporation broke into the phototypesetting machinery market with a series of new devices at the exhibition PRINT 68 in Chicago. Prices of the machines were unprecedentedly and unimaginably low. Popularisation of phototypesetting techniques and the demise of hot-metal methods were accelerated by these events. Most notable of the new machines were the CG2961 and CG4961. Incorporated in the hard-wired logic of the units was the ability to justify and hyphenate text, thereby advancing the concept of the 'intelligent' phototypesetter (see 1966). Value engineering was applied as straightforward, unfussy and inexpensive. Operator intervention was frequently necessary to change photo-matrices incorporated on a film strip (for style and size), width plugs, and set gears.

PTS   Compugraphic Corporation announced the CG7200 keyboard-operated headlining machine. No fewer than 1,000 of the units had been installed by 1970.

abcdefghijklmnopqrstu
ABCDEFGHIJKLMNOP
1234567890 .,;:'"«»&!

Caxton

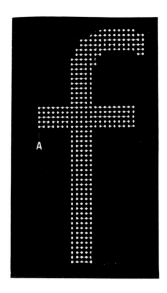

Digitised character for the Fototronic CRT

KEY   Keycomp input perforators produced by Bouchery & Mincel to cut text tapes for Photon 713 phototypesetters.

CAT   HMSO completed developments for the composition of telephone directories by computer-controlled typesetting.

PTS   First Linotron 505 phototypesetter installed in the United Kingdom at Portsmouth & Sunderland Newspapers Ltd.

KEY   Automix Keyboards Inc. formed. It developed a range of input keyboards for driving particularly Linotype and Photon phototypesetters. Early models used Nixie tubes to record the assembly of a line, the numerical display telling at any given moment the amount of relative units remaining to be filled. At the back of the electric typewriter (for capturing alphanumerics) was a console standing vertically with six horizontal rows of rotary and toggle switches which enabled typographic formats to be set up consisting of leading, point size, type style, word-spacing limits, and line length. Once established, the formats could be summoned for automatic punching into paper tape.

VDU   A video editing unit (VDU) was first used for corrections in phototypesetting at Southwark Offset Ltd. in London. Conceptually the approach was uncomplicated and involved the perfecting of punched paper tape with a Cossor CoSprite DIDS 402 video display unit. In practice, the unjustified tapes produced at text-capturing keyboards were fed into the CoSprite which displayed the contents on the video screen for validation. Corrections were executed by cursor address. Output was a second and amended unjustified tape ready for passing on to phototypesetters. Nothing could have been simpler, but a landmark in phototypesetting history had been attained.

1969

LIN   Intertype Corporation discontinued manufacture of linecasters in the USA and centralised the activity in the United Kingdom.

TYP   Beatrice Warde died on 14 September.

PTS   Monophoto Filmsetter Mark 5 introduced. It offered greater flexibility in the distribution of inter-linear space than on previous models.

PTS   Photon Fontmaster 532 phototypesetting system revealed. In the photo-unit a couple of photo-matrix discs were incorporated with the light paths from each merged by optical elements. Typographic content of the machine amounted to a phenomenal 32 type styles and 24 sizes to yield 768 founts.

PTS   Debut of the Photon 713-100-15 phototypesetter, a machine extending the technical specification of an established family of products and using the same design principles. Increases of speed to 50 characters per second derived from exposing text over the forward and reverse traverses of the escapement carriage which scanned lines up to 15 inches long. Numbered among the enticements to purchase the machine was the possibility of outputting complete newspaper pages!

PTS   Monotype Studio-lettering Machine introduced, a device applying principles not dissimilar to a photographic enlarger and imaging from a photo-matrix disc.

PTS   Photon 713-200-15 phototypesetter announced. Rated at 100 characters per second, the upgraded productivity ensued from bidirectional carriage exposures, from continuous movement of the escapement carriage as distinct from stepping, and from repeated characters on the photo-matrix drum. Additionally the machine incorporated a Honeywell 112 minicomputer as a programmable controller. Such a concept was to develop rapidly and to eclipse hard-wired logic. In reality the Photon 713-200-15 existed more on paper than in hardware.

PTS   AM 707 phototypesetting machine released. It was developed and manufactured by Photon Inc. for sale by Addressograph-Multigraph.

Sketch of Beatrice Warde by Eric Gill

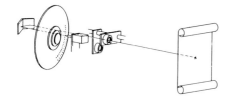

Optical system of the AM 707

Most notable technical feature of the unit was a system of optical leverage which escaped the width of a character prior to determining the size of the image, whereas the usual procedure was the other way around. In practice, the lens had the effect of optically magnifying the displacement as well as scaling and focusing the output character. Optical leverage was eventually applied with huge success in the Photon Pacesetter series of machines (see 1971).

PTS   Compugraphic Corporation purchased some significant phototypesetting patents from Walter Peery. They encompassed a couple of prime inventions for character escapement: the rotating mirror and the stepping lens.

PTS   Debut of the Singer Company in the phototypesetting market with the Justotext 70 machine. It was designed to accept 7-level counted input tapes compatible with the Justowriter strike-on composition system from the same supplier. In many respects the unit was imitative of the CG2961 and CG4961 devices (see 1968), a view later upheld in the courts following patent litigation by the Compugraphic Corporation against the Singer Company.

PTS   Monophoto 600 phototypesetter uncovered at the GEC exhibition in Milan, the first electronic machine to be produced by the Monotype Corporation. Founts were stored on a quartet of photo-matrix discs with 100 characters apiece supplemented by a turret of 200 pi-sorts in the form of 35mm. slides. Merging of the diverse light paths was performed optically. Justified 8-channel tapes constituted the text input to the machines. Quoted speed was 35 characters per second.

PTS   American Type Founders announced the Photocomp 20, a phototypesetter that failed to establish a foothold in the market.

PTS   Another newcomer to the phototypesetting machinery market emerged as Graphex Inc. offering a series of Typodyne units. Several novel features were embodied in the engineering such as a fibre-optics tube for conveying light from a source up to the face of a photo-matrix, a rotating optical periscope for collecting images from a stationary photo-matrix, and a curved sensitive plane to maintain focus across a text line as characters impinged from an oscillating mirror. In commercial terms, the Typodyne machines were utter failures.

PTS   Peter Purdy and Ronald McIntosh set up a joint company with Harris-Intertype, a collaboration which was to yield the budget-priced Fototronic 600 phototypesetter (see 1972).

PTS   Compugraphic Corporation charged that Singer Graphic Systems had contravened two of the patents of Walter Peery. Retaliation occurred in the ensuing year when GSI and Singer countersued Compugraphic claiming among other things 'violation of antitrust laws in ... obtaining certain patents'. Singer eventually compensated Compugraphic by paying an undisclosed sum.

VDU   Hendrix Electronics unveiled the Hendrix 5102FD video editing unit which was used by the Associated Press as a prototype. Seemingly the unit was afflicted by a myriad of technical problems.

TO   IBM coined the description Media Industry for activities involved with communications, whether electronic, oral, or paper-based.

1970

LIN   Mergenthaler Linotype Co. decided to terminate production of hot-metal linecasting machines in the USA. Some 90,000 units had been manufactured in the American plants.

LIN   Linotype Model 794 released. Designed for manual or tape operation, the machine had a rated speed of 12 newspaper lines per minute. Some ergonomic engineering had been undertaken to make the unit more convenient and faster to operate. It carried four magazines and had some relationship to the forerunning Linotype Model 79. This was the last Linotype linecasting machine to be announced in Britain.

MON At the end of the year a new high-speed composition mould was released for Monotype casters. Immediate increases in productivity of 3 per cent to 38 per cent were claimed on type sizes between 6 and 12 point.

MON Merger took place in the USA of the Lanston Monotype Co. and the American Type Founders Co.

SO Manufacture of the Justowriter strike-on composition system was discontinued. More than 19,000 units had been installed over the previous two decades. That number does not include the 1,100 machine chassis sold to American Type Founders for production of the ATF Typesetter (see 1958).

TYP International Typeface Corporation established in New York by Aaron Burns, Herb Lubalin, and Ed Rondthaler. It is a type-design agency which publishes a great deal of promotional material to support the new typefaces, including the quarterly magazine *U & 1c*. Some three to four type families are released annually; the first to appear in the founding year were Avant Garde Gothic by Herb Lubalin and Tom Carnase followed by Souvenir from Ed Benguiat based on earlier work by M. F. Benton (1914). Most composing equipment manufacturers licence designs from ITC. Many eminent designers have contributed to the ITC collection.

TF Konrad F. Bauer died on 17 March (see 1903).

PTS Linofilm VIP phototypesetter launched. Its structure incorporated a Microdata 810 minicomputer which acted simultaneously as a controller for the photo-deck and as a text processor for organising typographically the incoming unjustified data. It sounded the death knell for hard-wired front-end logic in a phototypesetter. Photo-matrices were mounted on an oscillating drum which stopped momentarily when a selected character came in front of a flash lamp. Character escapement was by a rotating mirror deflecting images on to a curved sensitive plane. For type sizing, a zoom lens system was employed.

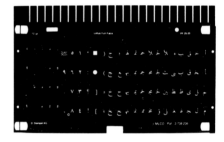

Linofilm VIP photo-matrix

PTS Mergenthaler Linotype GmbH uncovered the Linofilm Europa, a direct-entry phototypesetter. It was distinguished by a drum bearing 480 individual photo-matrix slides secured magnetically in four rows. Each matrix slide was configured with two characters, strobe timing information, and independent access codes. In operation the photo-matrix drum spun continuously, a stroboscopic flash picking off the desired characters. Zoom lenses did the image sizing and the escapement carriage sported the conventional collecting lens and mirror. The keyboard was an electric typewriter giving a hard copy proof.

PTS Photon Inc. charged that the Compugraphic Corporation had violated patents dealing with timing slits on a moving matrix for the selection of characters; with keyboard logic relating to line justification; and with storage of character widths on a printed circuit card. The Compugraphic Corporation countersued complaining that the Peery patents (see 1969) had been contravened. In 1971 an out-of-court settlement was concluded, Compugraphic agreeing to pay $1,000,000 to Photon in three annual instalments.

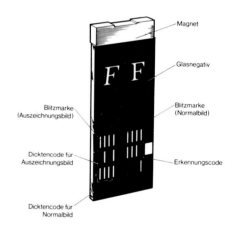

Photo-matrix for the Linofilm Europa

PTS In November Photon Inc. filed a suit against the Alphatype Corporation for alleged transgression of a widths card patent and a keyboard logic patent. It was an action never brought to trial because the defendant agreed that reparation of $250,000 should be paid to the plaintiff.

PTS Harris Corporation announced the Fototronic TxT, a phototypesetter incorporating a Varian 520 minicomputer. In certain respects the machine perpetuated the technical principles of the Fototronic 480 (see 1964) and Fototronic 1200 (see 1968). Nonetheless the new model did embody changes. It deployed a lens turret and not zoom optics for type sizing; the escapement was by oscillating mirror with an associated field-flattening lens and not by film-carriage movement;

and the character widths resided in the memory of the minicomputer with the optical values on the photo-matrix disregarded.

PTS Star Parts Co. came into the phototypesetting machinery market with the CompStar 150 unit. It output hyphenless justified text from non-counted input tapes, ran at a speed of 75 characters per second, and carried a modest price tag. Engineering design was unoriginal and embodied established techniques. Character escapement emanated from a rotating mirror, but niceties of field flattening were ignored to keep costs down. Later in the year, the CompStar 190 machine surfaced with a slightly more endowed typographic specification.

PTS Singer Company brought to market a second machine called the Photomix 70 with a hard-wired logic pack at the front-end encompassing line justification and rudimentary word hyphenation routines. Graphic Systems Inc. designed and built the unit. Original aspects of the machine embraced a fibre-optics pipe which conducted stroboscopically-formed images from a sizing lens right up to the sensitive plane and served as a means of character escapement. Secondly a photo-matrix drum accommodated four type styles as individual quadrants which provided complete freedom in typographic dressing of the machine.

PTS Linotron 505C phototypesetter released, the C standing for computer. It reflected the trend of the time with a minicomputer controller being configured as part of the machine (viz. Honeywell 316) replacing the earlier hard-wired logic. In some respects, the development was presaged by the work of the research team for computer typesetting at Newcastle University under the leadership of the late John Duncan which had successfully interfaced a Digico Micro 16 to the photo-unit. With a minicomputer in residence, a number of software packages were written for the Linotron 505C by Linotype-Paul Ltd. Initially a CORA I program was developed which assumed the functions of the erstwhile hard-wired controller.

PTS IBM withdrew from the CRT typesetting market (see 1967).

FES Digital Equipment Corporation heralded the PDP-11 computer which acted as the centrepiece for many clustered multi-terminal composition systems. Its Unibus architecture facilitated the servicing of numerous on-line peripheral devices without overloading the central processing unit.

PTS Autologic Inc., the purveyor of the APS series of CRT phototypesetters, emerged as a separate commercial entity from its parent Alphanumeric Inc.

KEY Maltron I keyboard devised, consisting of a normally arranged bank of keys, except that a noticeable separation occurs between the left-hand and right-hand assignments permitting the operator to hold the hands in more natural and comfortable positions. Also the arrangement of characters differs considerably from the customary QWERTY.

OCR ECRM Inc. was established.

OCR ECRM Inc. uncovered the Autoreader optical character recognition machine for scanning typescripts prepared in the founts Courier 12, OCR A, and OCR B. It was marketed for the uncustomarily low price of $89,000. Scanning was accomplished by a half-dozen vidicon tubes. Recognition logic secured a match between a scanned and an idealised character within given parameters of variance and made the appropriate output. Scanning speed was rated at 700 words per minute. Control was exercised by a PDP-8E computer. Some editing on the typescripts was permissible.

VDU Harris 1100 video editing unit disclosed. To most industrial observers, the machine really established the criteria to be attained in video editing, especially for the quality and stability of the display. As a stand-alone device, the Harris 1100 simply served to perfect punched paper tapes. Capacity of the screen was 2,000 characters with a buffer memory to match in the standard machine, but expandable by option. Hard-wired logic was encased by the unit.

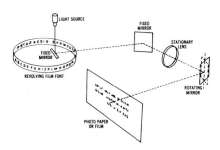

Optical system of CompStar 150

1971

LIN   Ludlow Typograph Co. acquired Sasmats Ltd. and formed Ludlow Industries (UK).

TF   Bauer Giesserei (typefoundry) closed operations in Frankfurt, but resumed trading as Fundicion Tipografica Neufville in Barcelona.

J&P   *The Primer for Computer Composition* by John W. Seybold was published.

J&P   *The Seybold Report* on composition systems was launched. It grew in reputation to become compulsory reading for the cognoscenti.

PTS   Dymo Industries Inc. acquired the Star Parts Co.

PTS   Compugraphic Corporation unleashed the CompuWriter, the earliest inexpensive direct-entry phototypesetter. It gained immediate acceptance by the printing industry.

PTS   Photon Pacesetter phototypesetting machine surfaced consisting of 26 different models. In essence the machine accommodated either a 4-style or 8-style photo-matrix disc functioning in conjunction with from four to sixteen pre-sized focusing lenses. Accordingly the machines accommodated from 16 to 128 typographical variations under automatic keyboard control. From an engineering standpoint, the machine was remarkable for a system of optical leverage whereby the escapement for a character occurred in advance of image sizing, a reversal of normal procedures (see 1969).

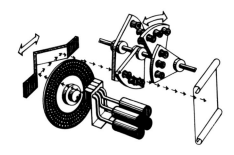

Pacesetter optical system

PTS   Addressograph-Multigraph released the AM 747 phototypesetting machine, a more automated version of the forerunning AM 725 (see 1967). Elements in the optical system were adjusted under automatic control exercised through a Varisystems P16 minicomputer. Input of unjustified data tapes was permissible, an improvement over its predecessor.

PTS   AM 744 phototypesetter unveiled by Addressograph-Multigraph, a machine based on the architecture of the Photon Pacesetter deploying optical leverage and an integral Varisystems P16 minicomputer. The AM 744 provided exchangeable type sizing lenses, whereas those on the Photon Pacesetter were fixed.

PTS   Compugraphic Corporation divulged the ACM 9000 and 9001 phototypesetters: the former operated directly from a keyboard and the latter functioned from punched paper tape input. Both units incorporated 8 type styles and a dozen point sizes aggregating to 96 typographical variations.

PTS   Magnaset 226 phototypesetter uncovered by Crosfield Electronics Ltd. Founts were stored as photo-matrices on a spinning drum, the selection of a character occurring by stroboscopic flash. The character was projected on to the face of an image orthicon tube and scanned, the video data being used to reconstitute the form on an output CRT. Characters were not generated in text sequence, but in order of convenience and availability from the photo-matrix drum. Control of the machine was by a PDP-8 computer which established positioning co-ordinates for the characters as generated within an area on the output CRT. The machine did not succeed.

PTS   Dr.-Ing. Rudolf Hell organisation became part of Siemens AG, the giant German computer group.

PTS   RCA withdrew from the graphic systems business, the custody of the Videocomp line of phototypesetters (see 1965) passing to Information International Inc.

PTS   Autologic Inc. (successor to Alphanumeric Inc.) revealed the APS-4 digital CRT phototypesetter. In the same year a marketing pact was concluded with Photon Inc. for the machine to be distributed as the Photon 7000.

PTS   Seaco 1600 cathode ray tube phototypesetter surfaced. It was an unsuccessful foray into the technology, though a fundamental design postulation involved the storage of digital founts as outline forms in contradistinction to run-length coding applied previously. Several advantages attached to the outline technique, such as the more economic occupation of computer memory because a single character master could be employed for a series of type sizes, and a standard output resolution could be achieved safeguarding quality of character definition over a series of point sizes.

OCR Compuscan 170 optical character recognition (OCR) page reader was announced at $55,000, a good deal less expensive than the ECRM Autoreader (see 1970). It scanned by moving the document beneath a photo-diode array which sensed the black and white patterns and converted the samplings to digital forms for the recognition logic. Several typewriter founts could be read, including Courier 12, Perry, OCR A, and OCR B. Scanning speed was quoted as 750 words per minute. Integral to the machine for running the recognition logic was a Data General Nova 1200 computer. Operator assistance to identify dubious characters could be solicited. Considerable post-recognition logic was encompassed by the machine for code translation strings and the like.

VDU Hendrix 5200 video editing unit superseded the earlier and troublesome 5102FD (see 1969) from the same supplier. Systems philosophy of the Hendrix 5200 matched precisely that of the preceding CoSprite (see 1968), namely a stand-alone device that accepted punched paper tape, displayed its contents on a CRT screen for proofing and correction, and generated a second tape. Logic of the Hendrix 5200 was hard-wired.

VDU Mergenthaler Linotype Co. divulged the CorRecTerm M100, a video editing unit designed to expunge errors from punched paper tapes. Its screen and buffer memory accommodated 1,920 characters. Logic of the unit was hard-wired.

VDU Composer 15 video editing unit brought out by the Imlac Corporation. It was a device that bristled with original features. Firstly the machine was software based on a PDS-1 computer. Secondly the display characters were created from vector strokes and by software, instead of the more usual dot matrix in MOS chips. Thirdly the video display was refreshed from core memory and not from MOS chips as on most concurrent devices. Fourthly the unit incorporated justification and hyphenation logic which could be employed interactively by the operator. Fifthly the display characters were proportionally spaced, as distinct from monospaced founts on competitive devices. Sixthly the screen display simulated justified and hyphenated text with a straight right margin and could display characters in four different and user-selectable sizes.

FES Installation of the first clustered front-end composition system occurred in the *News Journal* at Daytona Beach. It was developed by Xylogics Inc. Nucleus of the system was the GRI-909 computer with 16K of 16-bit memory which co-ordinated interaction between the various peripherals through a central universal bus. Peripherals included a half-dozen on-line IBM and Facit typewriters for data input, a 500Mb. magnetic disc for text storage, and a quartet of on-line Delta Data Telterm video editing screens. Output was to a couple of paper tape punches.

FES Embryonic version of the more mature Ferranti CS5 and CS7 Systems was installed at the *Scottish Daily Record*.

1972

LIN Matrotype Ltd. (see 1965) purchased by Kreiter Brothers, the same interest that bought the Chicago Type Foundry.

PTS Fairchild Graphic Systems assimilated by the Addressograph-Multigraph Corporation. Fairchild had been a pioneer in the development of teletypesetting keyboards and control units, computer composition systems, and later diversified with lesser effect into phototypesetting.

TYP *The Times* newspaper of London appeared on 9 October for the first time in the Times Europa typeface designed by Walter Tracy (see 1947) of Linotype- Paul Ltd.

TF Deberny & Peignot typefoundry acquired by Haas'sche Schriftgiesserei.

PTS Laser substituted for the xenon flash lamp in a Photon 560 phototypesetter (see 1962) to enable exposure of images on to dry silver materials. Such a concept dispensed with wet chemical processing of the latent image. Instead the application of heat was necessary. It was an unsuccessful scheme.

PTS CompuWriter International and Universal I and II direct-entry phototypesetters released by the Compugraphic Corporation. Prices were unimaginably low for the time, a CompuWriter International selling for £3,450 and a Universal II for £5,650. Essentially the photo-units were identical to those of the CG2961 and CG4961 machines (see 1968). Feedback of information to the operator at the integral keyboard embraced a marching display of the last 32 characters tapped and a decremental numeric display of the line length remainder.

PTS Several improvements were implemented for the Linofilm VIP phototypesetter: (a) an increase in running speed to 25 characters per second, (b) an extended measure from 36 to 45 picas, (c) an alternative of one, two, or three fount drums (i.e. 6, 12, or 18 type styles) with the image paths from each merged optically by a pentaprism, (d) a choice of size ranges from 6 to 48 or 72 point, and (e) an increase in computer memory up to 12K bytes.

PTS Mark 2 version of the Photon Pacesetter phototypesetting machine brought to market. It ran at a brisker speed of 45 characters per second realised by spinning the photo-matrix disc faster and by niftier movements of the escapement carriage. By reducing the number of type styles on the photo-matrix and by repeating characters of high frequency in the locations vacated, a speed of 75 characters per second could be coaxed from the machine.

PTS AM 744 and 748 phototypesetters introduced with the proprietary Amtrol minicomputer serving at the front end as a replacement for the Varisystems P16. Both units applied the principle of optical leverage for character imaging and laydown; the difference was in the number of type-sizing lenses accommodated of four and eight respectively.

PTS Photon Inc. alleged that Graphic Systems Inc. and Singer Graphic Systems, with the Photomix 8000 machine, had transgressed its patents for storing character widths on a printed circuit card, for using timing slits on a rotating photo-matrix, and for calculating character escapement values over a range of type sizes. In 1974 the two defendants agreed to compensate the complainant with $350,000 before a court judgement had been reached.

PTS H. Berthold AG released the Diatronic S, a tape-driven version of an earlier direct-entry phototypesetter bearing the same name (see 1967).

PTS Photon Inc. sued H. Berthold AG for breach of phototypesetting patents and eventually received an out-of-court settlement.

PTS Photon Compositor launched, an unconvincing direct-entry phototypesetter consisting of a keyboard lashed up to a Pacesetter exposure unit (see 1971).

PTS Fototronic 600 revealed by Harris-Intertype. Designed by Peter Purdy and Ronald McIntosh, the machine employed a spinning photo-matrix disc and selectively imaged characters by stroboscopic flash. Lateral spacing of characters in a text line was by way of a traversing optical carriage. Control logic was hard-wired. Development policy differences between the American and British branches of the manufacturer ensured that the machine did not enjoy commercial success.

PTS Bobst Graphic Systems entered the phototypesetting machinery market with the Eurocat, a model designed by Graphic Systems Inc. and embodying a Data General Nova 1210 minicomputer.

abcdefghijklmnopqrstu
ABCDEFGHIJKLMNO
1234567890 .,;:"«»&!?

Times Europa

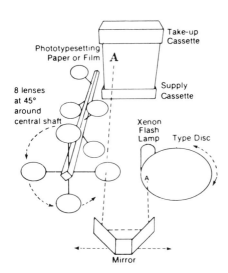

Optical system for the AM 748

Photo-matrix disc for Fototronic 600

PTS Linotron 505TC phototypesetter inaugurated, a machine that generated text on both the outward and inward travels of the print-out lens, as opposed to the unidirectional composition practised previously. The development effectively doubled the speed of the unit to around 300 newspaper lines per minute. *TC* in the designation stood for *Two-way Computer-controlled*.

PTS Crosfield Electronics Ltd. sold the Magnaset 226 phototypesetter development project (see 1971) to the Sun Chemical Co. in the USA. The machine was re-named the Sunsetter. Additionally an endeavour was made to substitute digital founts for the large photo-matrix drum, but the efforts came to nought in the commercial sense.

PTS MGD Graphic Systems Division of Rockwell International entered the phototypesetting market by unveiling the Metro-Set cathode ray tube machine. It successfully applied the storage of digital founts as outlined shapes (see 1971) and for output used a CRT complete with a fibre-optic faceplate which came into direct contact with the photosensitive material. Speeds in excess of 1,000 newspaper lines per minute could be obtained. Alternative output resolutions were offered at 496, 744, and 1,488 lines per inch. Measures up to 66 picas and type sizes up to 72 point could be accomplished. Control of the machine was exercised by an integral Data General Nova 1200 computer.

GRA Digigraph scanner developed by Dr.-Ing. Rudolf Hell for inputting digitised graphics (e.g. logotypes) to a composition system for eventual output to a CRT typesetter.

PTS Information International Inc. took over the Videocomp and related interests of RCA.

PTS Kodak introduced resin-coated (RC) sensitive paper for phototypesetting: a more stable and permanent alternative to the preceding stablisation materials.

TYP *Specification for Metric Typographic Measurement* issued by the British Standards Institution. It has been largely ignored.

KEY Varisystems Corporation established. It introduced the first keyboard to encompass a CRT display which blurred the distinction that had previously existed between stand-alone video editing units and input keyboards. In concept the Varicomp 2000 and 3000 units were built on a modular principle, the modules involved being: a non-counting keyboard with paper tape punch (the Varicomp 2000), a CRT display, a P16 minicomputer with 8K bytes for counting and other logic, and a punched paper tape reader. Various keyboard configurations could be assembled from the modules.

OCR ECRM Inc. reduced the price of the original Autoreader 700 (see 1970) from $89,000 to $69,500 and released the faster Autoreader 1200 for $79,500: the 1200 designation referring to words scanned per minute.

OCR MGD Graphic Systems joined the ranks of suppliers of optical page readers with a machine developed and manufactured by Cognitronics Inc. It used a helium-neon laser as the light source and a photo-diode array as the scan sensor. Typewriter founts recognised were OCR A, OCR B, and Courier 12. Originally a PDP-8 computer served as the controller later to be replaced by a Data General Nova 1200 central processor. Graphic Systems Inc. and its European surrogate Bobst Graphic Systems SA marketed a specially-packaged version of the same machine.

VDU Omnitext developed a stand-alone video editing terminal which started the practice of defining an element of copy (e.g. a paragraph, line, sentence, etc.) before operating upon it, a fail-safe practice that has become a commonplace.

FES Harris Corporation introduced a video terminal that came nearer to simulating the finished printed result by displaying type close to the intended point size, by displaying lines to the correct typeset length, and by displaying accurate inter-linear spacing. One stick-figure fount was employed to represent all type styles. In addition, the Harris 2200 display was interactive and did enable the dynamic determination of typesetting parameters automatically by program. As originally configured, the Harris 2200 system consisted of a quartet of terminals on-line to a PDP-11 computer.

FES   IBM and a number of large North American newspaper publishers formed the Newspaper Systems Development Group. The aim was to define and to develop a total newspaper composition system capable of producing complete pages with integrated text and graphics.

FES   First use of the term *floppy disc* occurred to describe an external magnetic computer memory formed on a flexible plastic base.

FES   Digital Equipment Corporation used its own PDP-11 computer as the foundation for the Typeset-11 composition system, a growing trend among competitive vendors in the industry.

FES   Harris 2500 composition system released. Central to the product was a PDP-11 computer equipped with eight multiplexors each accepting four terminals; as a consequence the configuration could be expanded to 32 terminals with a single CPU. Input of text was by a cluster of Harris 1500 video typewriters. Text was stored on a fixed-head magnetic disc for retrieval at Harris 1100 terminals where heavy editing could take place. Other on-line peripherals were phototypesetters, wire service lines, paper tape punches, and magnetic tape transports.

FES   Hendrix Electronics Inc. joined the growing ranks of companies developing multi-terminal front-end composition systems. It disclosed the Hendrix 3400 system based on a PDP-11/35 controller. Up to fifteen Hendrix 5700 terminals could be connected on-line. Characteristic of the system was intelligence centralised in the PDP-11 computer with supplicant terminals functioning as satellites.

FES   Early use of the term *front-end processor* for computer systems occurred in the *Scientific American* and in the *Dictionary of New English* (Barnhart).

1973

TYP   Gunter Gerhard Lange appointed type director for H. Berthold AG. He has been responsible for a vigorous development programme of original typefaces, as well as for licensing and adapting designs from other sources. His own designs include: Concorde (1969), Berthold Script (1977), and Imago (1982).

PTS   The Monotype Corporation Ltd. was the subject of two insensitive commercial takeovers.

TYP   *Vienna Agreement for the Protection of Type Faces and their International Deposit* was drafted by the World Intellectual Property Organisation and signed by ten countries after much lobbying and preparatory work by the Association Typographique Internationale (A.Typ.I). It awaits ratification by five countries before coming into international effect.

PTS   Compugraphic Corporation introduced the MagSet record/playback system using magnetic tape cassettes for text storage. It was designed for application with the Universal II direct-entry phototypesetter (see 1972). MagSet was the first record/playback system devised for direct-entry equipment.

PTS   Linocomp direct-entry phototypesetter uncovered by the Linotype Group of Companies. It had been engineered to a low price of £5,300, as evidenced by the crudities of two levers flanking the keyboard for activating mechanical linkages to alter type size and type style respectively. Text feedback to the operator was by a 32-character self-scan display. Justification data took the form of a numerical read-out of the line length remainder. Individual filmstrips for four type styles were held on a drum. Character selection occurred by stroboscopic flash. Two pre-focused lenses determined point size of the image. Character escapement was by a rotating mirror.

abcdefghijklmnopqrst
ABCDEFGHIJKLMN
XYZ 1234567890 .,;:'"

Concorde

Linocomp 1

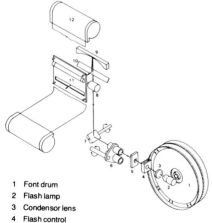

1   Font drum
2   Flash lamp
3   Condensor lens
4   Flash control
5   Aperture
6   Exposure optics
    Linocomp 1: switchable to 2 type sizes
7   Turning mirror (with drive system)
8   Film advance motor
9   Concave mirror
10 Light beam distributor (translucent mirror)
11 Exposure plane
12 Output cassette

PTS   Mark 3 version of the Photon Pacesetter phototypesetting machine announced with 16 type styles in residence, a doubling of the previous highest capacity.

PTS   Singer Company upgraded the Photomix 8000 series of phototypesetters by a Model 8400 embracing a Data General Nova 1210 minicomputer consistent with the machine architecture of the time.

PTS   Monophoto 400/31 launched. It was an odd amalgam of mechanics, fluidics, and electronics. Text was input as justified 31-channel tapes in the traditional manner of the Monotype Corporation Ltd. Photo-matrices consisted of 400 individual characters encased as a grid. Speed rating was 40,000 characters per hour.

PTS   Compugraphic Corporation unveiled the Videosetter, a CRT phototypesetter value engineered to a budget price in the best traditions of the supplier. It stored founts on a single photo-matrix grid and a character was selected from an array of 108 by an image dissector. Output was by way of a CRT tube fitted with a fibre-optic faceplate. One line of text was generated at a time on the imaging tube. The photosensitive material came into direct contact with the tube and dispensed with the need for a projection lens. Measure was limited to 27 picas and the maximum point size to 36. Output speed was 400 to 500 newspaper lines per minute at a resolution of 1,300 lines per inch. Typographic variations were obtained by electronic modulation of the founts.

PTS   Linotron 505TC-100 announced. Instead of the imaging CRT remaining stationary as on earlier models with a moving lens providing displacement for the scan lines, the Linotron 505TC-100 involved the travel of a small CRT over a carriageway stretching to 100 picas. In effect, the CRT generated successive scan lines in a constant position on the tube and the travel furnished the displacement. The 100 picas specification served as an enticement to the electronic make-up of broadsheet newspaper pages.

PTS   Linotron 303 phototypesetter introduced as a replacement for the Linotron 505. The new machine employed principles similar to its progenitor for character generation, though greatly rationalised in execution. It involved a flying spot scan of photo-matrices with the characters written out on to the sensitive plane by a travelling CRT. Control and composition programs ran in an integral Prime 100 computer with memory options extending from 4 to 64K.

VDU   Automix Keyboards Inc. brought out the UltraComp range of input and editing equipment based on a microprocessor. It was one of the first applications of the new computing technology in the printing industry. In addition to punched paper tape, a Philips-style magnetic tape cassette was offered for text storage.

OCR   Compuscan Alpha optical character recognition machine launched. It utilised a photo-diode array for scanning which oscillated across the documents. Initially the reading speed was 350 words per minute later accelerated to 600 and 1,200. Editing and correcting of documents could be practised in accordance with strict conventions. Perry, Courier 12, and OCR B typewriter founts came within the compass of the machine.

OCR   ECRM Inc. announced the Autoreader 5000 optical character recognition machine. It utilised a photo-diode read head for scanning documents in conjunction with a helium-neon laser deflected across a typewritten line by an oscillating mirror. Integral to the unit was a PDP-8 computer exercising the recognition logic.

OCR   Hendrix Electronics Inc. announced the OCR 1 system by Xicon Data Entry.

VDU   Coltec P-501 video editing unit devised, a stand-alone machine for ridding paper tape of errors. It was an early exponent of storing the display character shapes in RAM, thereby providing some facilities for the user to customise fount schemes on the CRT screen. Rights to the

Linotron 303 photo-matrix grid

unit were acquired by the Linotype Group of Companies prompting appearance of the Linoscreen.

FES   Atex Inc. founded by Charles and Richard Ying and by Douglas Drane to develop and to market front-end composition systems. Hardware configurations were based on the PDP-11 computer serving as a central repository of intelligence as explained for the Hendrix 3400 system (see 1972). First major customer for the fledgeling Atex Inc. was *US News and World Report,* while an early British user was the *Rochdale Observer.*

FES   Linotype Group of Companies expanded the Prime 100 computer system integral to the Linotron 505 and 303 phototypesetters with on-line video terminals. System V, as the configuration was labelled, became a considerable influence in the European composition marketplace, especially for newspaper production.

FES   Press Computer Systems Ltd. entered the front-end composition market with an equipment configuration based on the PDP-11 computer. It was a multi-terminal classified advertising and typesetting system and one of the first to integrate many of the overhead administrative functions associated with the production of newspaper advertising. Site of the initial installation was the *Express and Star* at Wolverhampton.

1974

TYP   Adrian Williams inaugurated Fonts, a type-design agency responsible for creating several distinguished and popular alphabets, such as Raleigh (1977), Leamington (1978), Seagull (1978), Accolade (1979), and Congress (1980). Numerous phototypesetting machinery manufacturers have licensed designs from Fonts.

TYP   Ikarus type-design system developed by Dr. Peter Karow. It enables a number of functions: (1) the conversion of scanned digital images to vectored outlines, (2) the conversion of analogue artwork to digital data, and (3) the interpolation of basic letter designs to yield a family of different weights, outlines, contours, etc. Several leading phototypesetting machine manufacturers have used the system for preparing digital type libraries, such as the Compugraphic Corporation and the Linotype Group of Companies.

TYP   Jan Tschichold died on 11 August (see 1902 and 1928). He designed several typefaces instanced by Transito (1931), Saskia (1932), and notably Sabon (1964): the last named was developed for universal application as founders' type, linecasting, and Monotype composition and a version is used for the text face of this book. In 1933 he designed about a dozen faces for the Uhertype photocomposing system, but none has been traced. His re-styling of Penguin Books in the late 1940s was another remarkable achievement among many others.

TYP   Maximilien Vox died on 18 December (see 1894). He devised a system of type-design classification in 1954 which has been widely accepted and applied.

PTS   After several years of tribulation, Photon Inc. finally plunged into bankruptcy, a sad occasion as the company had pioneered second-generation phototypesetting. Vestiges of the organisation were to be salvaged (see 1975), thereby perpetuating an innovative thread of history.

KEY   Varisystems Corporation filed for protection under Chapter 11 of the American bankruptcy code.

PTS   Addressograph-Multigraph released the innovative Comp/Set 500 direct-entry phototypesetter. Prominent in the hardware configuration was a full-size video screen, a marked contrast to the miserly self-scan displays and miscellaneous numeric read-outs that characterised equivalent phototypesetters. The video screen was invaluable. It exhibited text in the line currently being keyboarded, as well as the text in the line previously committed to the photo-deck. It

abcdefghijklmnopqrstu
ABCDEFGHIJKLMNOPQR
1234567890 .,;:''«»&!?

Seagull

abcdefghijklmnopqrstuv
ABCDEFGHIJKLMNO
Z 1234567890 123456

Sabon

displayed the functional status of the photo-unit, such as point size and line length. It allowed elementary video editing to occur.

PTS   Alphacomp direct-entry phototypesetter developed by the Alphatype Corporation. It was prematurely announced, though a few machines fitted with wire-wrapped boards reached the market and encountered reliability problems.

PTS   ExecuWriter introduced by the Compugraphic Corporation at PRINT 74 for under $4,000, the least expensive phototypesetter produced to date. It was aimed as a replacement for the strike-on equipment installed in the market. ExecuWriter II (a two-style as opposed to a single-style version) was unveiled soon afterwards.

PTS   Linocomp 2 direct-entry phototypesetter announced. It embodied several improvements over the Linocomp 1 (see 1973), such as five type-size lenses as opposed to two, firmware logic (ROM) and an Intel 8080 microprocessor as distinct from previous hard-wired logic, and the option of a record/playback system using punched paper tape for the storage of keystrokes. Most direct-entry phototypesetters of the period incorporated hard-wired logic with routines for automatic hyphenless line justification: the Linocomp 1 and 2 were not exceptions.

PTS   Mark 4 version of the Photon Pacesetter phototypesetting machine emerged with the refinement of reverse leading.

PTS   Running speed of Linofilm VIP further accelerated to 40 characters per second, an improvement traceable to the omission of mechanical shutters and to the adoption of multiple light sources with fibre optics for confining light to a given character.

PTS   Econosetter announced by Photon Inc., an outcrop of the forerunning direct-entry Photon Compositor machine (see 1972).

PTS   Monophoto 400/8 introduced, a machine perpetuating the optical and architectural principles of the preceding Monophoto 400/31 (see 1973), but demanding input of 8-channel tapes.

PTS   Videosetter 2414 emerged as an improvement on the pilot machine of 1973 (q.v.). It accommodated a pair of photo-matrix grids and output over an extended point size range.

PTS   Videocomp 500 phototypesetter ushered on to the market by Information International Inc.: the company acquired rights to the basic machine design from RCA (see 1972).

PTS   Eocom exhibited the prototype of a laser platemaker.

KEY   Varicomp 2100 keyboard divulged by the Varisystems Corporation. Unlike the earlier hard-wired Varicomp 2000 unit, the new model incorporated an Intel 8008 microprocessor and a RAM character generator.

VDU   Unified Composer stand-alone terminal promoted by the Compugraphic Corporation. It was intended for the inputting, editing, and composing of text.

FES   Camex instituted to develop and ultimately to market a terminal for composing and making-up displayed advertisements (see 1975).

FES   Raycomp 100 graphic terminal for the make-up of displayed advertisements entered the market. Configured around an Interdata processor with 64K of memory, the system could support up to four on-line terminals. Each workstation consisted of a video display which emulated the finished printed advertisement in terms of point size, inter-linear spacing, horizontal positioning, and justification/hyphenation. Additionally, video versions of roman and italic were exhibited. The Raycomp 100 terminal was a byproduct of the NSDG project (see 1972).

FES   Computer Composition Inc. joined the providers of text management systems. Hardware configuration was shaped around a Data General Nova computer supporting video terminals. Software emphasis was on commercial printing applications.

FES   Computype entered the budget-priced multi-terminal systems market with a Compustor configuration intended for newspaper production.

FES   Digital Equipment Corporation augumented the PDP-8 composition systems with video terminals (see 1966).

FES   Imlac Corporation graduated to a multi-terminal Composer 1500 system with a cluster of four workstations based on the PDS-1 computer (see 1971).

FES   MGD Graphic Systems augmented its Metroset CRT phototypesetter and Metroreader OCR page scanner with a newly-launched front-end composition system.

FES   Newspaper Electronics Corporation swelled the growing ranks of vendors of multi-terminal composition systems.

FES   One Systems entered the multi-terminal newspaper composition market. It had a faltering beginning, but ponderously recovered.

CAT   Penta Systems (see 1967) elected to sell its in-house composition development to outside companies, the first being the Maryland Composition Company. It was a powerful batch-processing system for general commercial printing applications based on the Data General Nova computer.

1975

PTS   Bill Garth, a joint founder with Ellis Hanson of the Compugraphic Corporation, died on 11 April.

TYP   Sir Francis Meynell died on 9 July (see 1891). His major achievement was the establishment with Vera Mendel and David Garnett of the Nonesuch Press in 1923. It issued a range of fastidiously designed and styled books produced by the best printing houses. Appointed Honorary Typographic Adviser to HMSO in 1945 and knighted in 1946.

PTS   Dymo Industries Inc. bought the assets of the bankrupt Photon Inc. (see 1974) and merged the acquisition with Star Parts (see 1971) to form Dymo Graphic Systems.

PTS   Singer Company deserted the typesetting market. Its Photomix phototypesetters were made by Graphic Systems Inc. which continued in business and perpetuated the original version of the machines. Omnitext terminals (see 1972) were another product in the Singer portfolio.

PTS   Sun Chemical Co. precipitately abandoned the typesetting market and jettisoned the Sunsetter output device (see 1972) and the Suncom front-end system.

PTS   Punched paper tape module added to the Comp/Set 500 (see 1974). It enabled keystrokes to be captured and stored on paper tape for ultimate playback through the video screen for editing. As a consequence, the humble concept of a direct-entry phototypesetter was expanded into a fully-fledged composition system.

PTS   Universal IV direct-entry phototypesetter emerged from the Compugraphic Corporation. It had a typographic complement equal to the ACM 9000 (see 1971), but encased a different and more efficient optical system.

PTS   Diatext phototypesetter promoted by H. Berthold AG, a simpler and less expensive companion to the Diatronic from the same supplier.

PTS   Copytronic direct-entry phototypesetter promoted by the Dr. Boger organisation. It was not a successful venture and an eventual takeover of the machine by Guttinger SA failed to salvage the project.

PTS   Compugraphic Corporation disclosed a Unisetter phototypesetter, a machine with eight type styles and a dozen point sizes. Unlike concurrent competitive machines, the front-end logic of the Unisetter was fashioned in firmware and did not comprise a programmable minicomputer.

PTS   Linotype Group of Companies became engaged in digital CRT typesetting through release of the Linotron 606, a top-of-the-line model in a freshly evolving family of machines. Owing to its high price, the Linotron 606 tended to remain exclusive.

PTS   Harris Corporation divulged a couple of high-speed CRT phototypesetters, the series 7400 and 7600.

PTS   Videosetter Universal revealed. It enhanced previous specifications in the family of machines by offering eight photo-matrix grids in residence, a stretched output line length to 45 picas, and an extended range of point sizes between 5 and 72.

PTS   IBM released the Model 3800 electronic printer. It was regarded more as a high-speed computer peripheral for a data processing environment, rather than as a graphic arts device.

GRA   ECRM Inc. announced the innovative Autokon 8400 electronic camera. Input hard copy consisted of line art and continous-tone photographs which were scanned, scaled, screened, and recorded on photosensitive material. Adjustments to tonal gradation were enabled by logic as well. Later, during the formative years of text and graphics integration, the Autokon served to input and to digitise pictures for storage on page make-up systems and acted as a raster scan output imaging device.

OCR   Compugraphic Corporation launched the Uniscan page reader manufactured by the Dest Data Corporation. It scanned stationary documents by means of a photo-diode strip constructed to the maximum line width occurring on a typewritten sheet. In operation the photo-diode strip simply travelled down the illuminated document collecting the necessary data at a phenomenally rated speed of 1,000 characters per second. Founts were restricted to Courier and OCR B. Fabrication was in hard-wired logic.

FES   Compuscan Inc. added to its line of OCR page scanners with the STaRT newspaper front-end system.

FES   Camex 135 graphic terminal surfaced on the market for the production of displayed advertisements. It was founded on a PDP-11/35 controller serving two workstations complete with explicit video display, graphic tablet, and keyboard.

FES   Linotype Group of Companies launched the PageView terminal as an adjunct to System V (see 1973).

FES   Quadex Corporation was inaugurated as a supplier of computer-based multi-terminal composition systems for general commercial printers.

1976

TYP   Bobst Graphic Systems issued its first original typeface Media designed by Andre Gurtler, Christian Mengelt, and Erich Gschwind.

PTS   Re-worked version of the Alphacomp direct-entry phototypesetter (see 1974) reached the market. It incorporated micro-programmed logic and an Intel 8080 microprocessor. Included in the machine was a self-scan display exhibiting to the operator the last 32 characters keyboarded. Reel-to-reel magnetic tape served to store keystrokes in the record/playback system. Optically the machine was simple, involving a fixed 3:1 light path with the photo-matrix effectively determining the output image size, while character escapement entailed movement of the lamp assembly and fount disc.

PTS   Floppy disc module offered with the Comp/Set 500 phototypesetter for the recording and playing back of keystrokes through the system (see 1974 and 1975).

PTS   Linotronic direct-entry phototypesetter introduced by Mergenthaler Linotype GmbH.

PTS   Quadritek 1200 direct-entry phototypesetter manifested by the Itek Corporation, a machine imitative in many respects of the Comp/Set 500 (see 1974). It had some original aspects, such as a photo-matrix disc fragmented into quadrants each bearing a type style, and a record/playback system deploying a magnetic tape cassette as the storage medium. It used a RAM-based program under microprocessor control. Feedback to the keyboard operator was by way of a full-blown video screen.

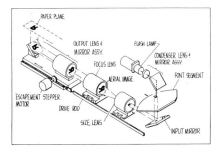

Quadritek optical system

PTS Linotype Group of Companies issued for the Linofilm VIP the Advanced Typography Program known by the shorthand ATP 1/54. In essence, the development introduced a system of 54 units to the em quad for calibrating founts and a sophisticated aesthetic program of kerning pair tables, of systematic white space adjustments between characters (i.e. tracking), of hung punctuation, of automatic ligature building, and of refined line justification. The program became a benchmark for imitations by many competitive suppliers.

PTS Monotype International revealed the Lasercomp, a digital laser phototypesetter. Unlike the ill-fated Dymo DLC-1000 machine that simulated a CRT method of building up characters by vertical stroking, the Lasercomp wrote out the text in raster fashion. That is the helium-neon beam was deflected by a spinning polygon mirror across the breadth of a page at 1,000 sweeps per inch. It was a significant development for the imaging of pages complete with text and graphics.

PTS DLC-1000 Composer, a digital laser phototypesetter, revealed by Dymo Graphic Systems. In certain respects the method of character generation was reminiscent of CRT techniques as seen in the vertical deflection of the laser beam juxtaposing strokes from a digital store to synthesise characters and lines of text.

KEY Maltron II keyboard announced. It involved not only a re-arrangement of characters from the traditional QWERTY, but a totally novel aspect to the placement of keybuttons. Instead of neat and regular rows of buttons built into inclined banks, the keys assumed an irregular and seemingly haphazard aspect. In fact, the arrangement was said to fit naturally with the hands and avoided any contortions and strains.

VDU MVP editing terminal announced by the Linotype Group of Companies as a complement to the Linofilm VIP.

FES Xenotron Ltd. formed to manufacture and to market the Xenotron Video Composer (see 1977).

FES Dissolution occurred of the Newspaper Systems Development Group (see 1972).

FES Automix Keyboards Inc. diversified into the multi-terminal composition business with the Maxi system. It was conceived for smaller-scale general commercial printers and newspapers.

FES Computer Composition Inc. (see 1974), a purveyor of front-end typesetting systems, experienced new ownership by Aarhus Stiftsbogtrykkerei of Denmark.

FES ECRM Inc. diversified into text management with the 7600 system, a hardware configuration based on the PDP-11 computer. Intelligence was lodged in the central control unit.

FES Harris Corporation took over Computype (see 1974), a merger of negligible impact in the marketplace.

FES Miles 33 established and became the British distributor for Penta Systems as well as developing specialist modules of software for the local market.

FES Mycro-Tek, a company inaugurated in 1974, delivered its first Mycro-Comp system to a newspaper. Distributed intelligence to terminal level was a feature of the system, as distinct from centralised intelligence in a controller favoured by some others.

FES Dymo Industries Inc. absorbed Xylogics Inc., an originator of multi-terminal text management systems (see 1971).

FES Shaffstall Corporation engaged in the marketing of floppy-disc conversion systems, an early manifestation of the need for typesetting equipment to interface with a variety of data capture, input, and processing devices.

1977

TYP Lettre d'Or competition for original type designs launched at the

Congress of the Association Typographique Internationale and sponsored by Bobst Graphic Systems. Winner announced in 1978 was Signa by Andre Gurtler, Christian Mengelt, and Erich Gschwind. Second prize went to Fontenay by Robert Flach and third came Meteora by Walter Sutter.

TYP Dr. Giovanni Mardersteig died on 27 December (see 1923).

J&P John W. Seybold published the book *Fundamentals of Modern Composition,* a valuable reference work.

PTS Linotype Group of Companies launched the Linoterm direct-entry phototypesetter at DRUPA. In essence the unit was an amalgam of two established products, namely the MVP Editing Terminal as front-end with the Linocomp 2 photo-unit as output. Foreground/background operations took place independently. At the time the Linoterm had the most comprehensive video display of any direct-entry phototypesetter and offered the most powerful text processing and handling routines (see 1974).

PTS Inauguration of the EditWriter 7500 direct-entry phototypesetter by the Compugraphic Corporation. It was a cardinal event at DRUPA. Hardware configuration consisted of a keyboard, a video screen (15 lines), a record/playback facility with dual floppy drives, and a photo-unit with 8 type styles, 12 point sizes, and a running speed of 25 characters per second. More significantly, the unit embodied a pair of Intel 8080 microprocessors. One microprocessor controlled operation of the photo-unit in background; while the other microprocessor served the keyboard, screen, and floppy drives in foreground. Two functions could proceed simultaneously. Powerful editing was another feature of the machine.

PTS Several extensions made to the Comp/Set product line with the introduction of the 3500 and 4500 series of machines. Running speed was increased three-fold to 25 characters per second; a range of floppy disc off-line video keyboards was introduced to capitalise on the speed through the separation of data capture; the number of resident photo-matrix discs could be optionally expanded to four, giving 16 type styles; and the composition logic was contained in RAM chips (not ROM as previously) and embraced automatic hyphenation.

PTS Based on a design by Louis Moyroud, a fresh incarnation of the Eurocat phototypesetter was released by Bobst Graphic Systems. It incorporated a spinning photo-matrix disc that presented characters speedily for stroboscopic selection and a pack of microlenses for creating a range of image sizes. In operation, the photo-matrix disc, xenon lamp, and lens pack travelled for escapement purposes along wayrods in front of the sensitive plane. The action was redolent of a golf-ball print head on a typewriter.

PTS Alphatype Corporation announced the Alphatype CRS digital phototypesetter. It took an uncomplicated approach by generating a single scan line on a 15 inch CRT tube, the displacement emanating from a moving lens. Microprocessing was entrusted to an Intel 8080 chip. Every point size had its own digital master stored in outline on multiple floppy diskettes. Reduction optics of 30:1 from the output tube furnished a resolution of 5,300 lines per inch on the sensitive plane over the size range 5 to 48 point. Speed was 80 newspaper lines per minute.

PTS Development of the DLC-1000 Composer (see 1976) was abandoned; a temporary setback for digital lasersetting.

PTS Xerox 9700 electronic printer revealed. Using electrophotographic methods of reproduction on to plain paper, the imaging was performed from a digital base on to a photoconductive surface with a laser deflected by a spinning polygon mirror. Originally the unit was perceived as a high-speed computer printer, but has gradually assumed greater significance for graphic arts' applications. Equipped with appropriate typographic founts, the Xerox 9700 becomes a combination of typesetter and demand printer. Founts from Linotype and other respected industrial sources have been licensed for use on the printers (see 1982).

FES   Compugraphic Corporation revealed the MDT 350 mini disc terminal.

FES   Xenotron Video Composer announced. It was an interactive display composition terminal offered at a price considerably lower than its competitive predecessors, such as the Harris 2200 (see 1972), the Raycomp 100 (see 1974), and the Camex 135 (see 1975). Basis of the stand-alone unit was an LSI-11 microcomputer. In concept the display depicted the finished printed result and functioned interactively. Establishment of composition parameters for output occurred dynamically by software. Unique to the Xenotron Video Composer was an area cursor which could be manipulated visibly on the screen to a given size and the copy spaced accordingly.

FES   Bedford Computer Corporation unveiled its Real Time Composition System built around the PDP-11 computer. One remarkable feature was the endeavour to simulate the finished printed appearance of the text on a bit map display and in real time.

FES   Digital Equipment Corporation launched the VAX-11/780, the first of a family of 32-bit computers.

1978

J&P   James Moran died on 24 February. He edited several trade journals, notably *Printing World,* and wrote several important books. Amongst the latter are numerous historical titles, such as *The Composition of Reading Matter* (1965), *Stanley Morison: His Typographic Achievement* (1971), and *Printing Presses* (1973).

TYP   ELF system of letter design based on computer technology proposed by David Kindersley and Neil Wiseman.

GRA   AM International took over ECRM Inc. and did very little to nurture and consolidate the acquisition.

PTS   Dymo Industries Inc. was assimilated by Esselte AB, the Swedish conglomerate.

PTS   MGD Graphic Systems retreated from the phototypesetting machinery market (see 1972).

SO   Manufacture of Varityper strike-on machines was discontinued.

TO   *Nottingham Evening Post* became the first newspaper in Britain to allow journalists to keyboard copy directly into a computerised composition system through the use of video terminals.

PTS   Peter Purdy and Ronald McIntosh developed the Spirascan method of editing digitised character outlines. Afterwards the co-ordinates of the outlines can be stored in a computer and later used for re-creating the images on a digital phototypesetter. Implementation of the system can be seen in the Comp/Edit digital phototypesetters manufactured by the Varityper Division of AM International.

PTS   AM International brought out the Comp/Edit 5810 direct-entry phototypesetter, a machine enabling foreground/background operations through the use of three microprocessors and a program resident in 80K of RAM memory. It sported the largest video editing screen to date in a direct-entry phototypesetter displaying 40 lines. Running speed was 25 characters per second. Four photo-matrix discs were deployed in the unit.

PTS   Compugraphic Corporation made known the EditWriter 7700 running at 40 characters per second, a quicker version of the EditWriter 7500 introduced the previous year. To exploit the increased speed and to occupy fully the background mode by capturing extra text off-line, a couple of input video keyboards surfaced as the EditWriter 1750 (non-counting) and EditWriter 2750 (counting).

PTS   Linotype Group of Companies introduced a couple of digital CRT phototypesetting machines to join the Linotron 606 (see 1975). First came the Linotron 404 followed a few months later by the more

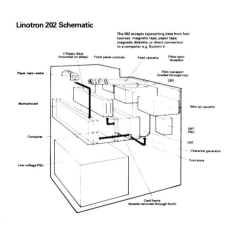

Schematic of Linotron 202
phototypesetter

significant Linotron 202 which attained pre-eminence in its served market sector. Using an output CRT with a fibre-optic faceplate, the digital founts were stored in outline as straight line vectors. Two were held in main memory with a further 60 on floppies. Characteristics encompassed a line length of 48 picas, a speed of 450 lines per minute, and a type size range from 4.5 to 72 point.

FES   Harris 2220 stand-alone graphics terminal released. It was an outcrop from the trail blazing Harris 2200 system of 1972 (q.v.).

FES   Compugraphic Corporation announced the AdVantage 5000 unit, a displayed advertisement composition terminal developed by Camex Inc. (see 1975).

FES   Key Corporation expanded still further the plethora of suppliers of text management systems by launching the Multiset III configuration.

OCR   Kurzweil Data Entry Machine (KDEM) emerged. It was an OCR page reader with omnifount capabilities accomplished by the machine creation of successive sets of digital character references.

1979

MC   Plus Printing Metals, a supplier of type alloys, ceased trading. It blamed closure on the decline of hot-metal typesetting which had contracted by 66 per cent over the previous ten years.

TYP   Donald Knuth developed the Metafont computerised design system for creating founts.

TYP   Reynolds Stone, the designer and wood-engraver, died on 23 June (see 1954).

PTS   Allied Chemical Corporation absorbed the Eltra Corporation: the Linotype Group of Companies constituted part of the latter conglomerate.

PTS   Esselte AB divested the Dymo Graphic Systems division (an amalgam of Star Parts, Photon, and Xylogics) to the Itek Corporation (see 1978).

PTS   Information International Inc. acquired the business interests of the MGD Graphic Systems Division.

PTS   Atex Inc. took over Automix Keyboards Inc., an apparently logical marrying of interests between vendors of large-scale and small-scale composition systems.

PTS   Bobst Graphic Systems absorbed the Varisystems Corporation (see 1972).

PTS   Wang Laboratories Inc. took over marketing of the Computer-Aided Typesetter (C/A/T) by Graphic Systems Inc.

FES   Key Corporation surrendered autonomy to the Alphatype Corporation (see 1978).

FES   Quadex Corporation (see 1975) bought by the Compugraphic Corporation, a liaison that has not been manifest in the product portfolios of European distributors.

PTS   Inception of the desk-top, direct-entry, and digital CRTronic phototypesetter by Mergenthaler Linotype GmbH. Configured with a keyboard, a video editing screen, and a pair of floppy disc drives for fount and text storage, the unit was most distinctive for the digital photo-unit. Founts were held on floppy disc coded in outline by vectors. Output of the digital forms was by way of a small travelling cathode ray tube (CRT). On the face of the CRT a single scan line was generated and as the continuous displacement occurred along a carriageway, the single scan lines were exposed side by side to synthesise the shapes of characters. Density of the lines was 1,270 per inch.

PTS   Omnitech 2000 direct-entry phototypesetter introduced by the Mergenthaler Linotype Co. It deployed digital founts stored as outlines. Imaging was by laser raster scan on to zinc oxide paper at 723 lines per inch, a galvanometer mirror served to deflect the laser beam across a page extending to 66 picas. In operation, the zinc oxide paper

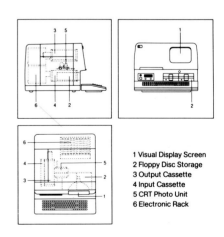

1 Visual Display Screen
2 Floppy Disc Storage
3 Output Cassette
4 Input Cassette
5 CRT Photo Unit
6 Electronic Rack

CRTronic phototypesetter

was wrapped around an internal cylinder of the machine. Next a corotron charge was applied to the paper followed by exposure to the laser which discharged the image areas. Toner was imparted to the image during a fourth revolution of the drum and final machine cycle. Industrial acceptance of the Omnitech 2000 was lukewarm.

PTS   Itek Corporation introduced the Mark VIII digital phototypesetter, a machine employing the escapement of roof mirrors in front of the character-generating CRT to span measures up to 100 picas. The unit was plagued by development problems.

PTS   Digiset 20T1 phototypesetter revealed by Dr.-Ing. Rudolf Hell. It was an attempt to moderate the price of a previously expensive family of machines.

PTS   Guttinger SA (see 1965), a Swiss supplier of text-processing equipment, diversified by introducing the GSA 789 digital CRT phototypesetter.

PTS   IBM 6670 laser printer entered the market.

VDU   Coltec Data Systems plunged into receivership.

PTS   Compugraphic Corporation introduced a version of the EditWriter 7500 phototypesetter (see 1977) that exposed characters on to a special photosensitive paper made by 3M. Development of the latent image was by the application of heat, instead of the wet processing necessitated by conventional materials. DryGraphic was the name given to the method. Photon Inc. had previously tried a similar scheme with laser exposure (see 1972). Other suppliers quickly emulated the Compugraphic example and adopted the same 3M paper. Quality of output was poor which led to market resistance and eventual failure.

FES   Somewhat belatedly, the Linotype Group of Companies entered the displayed advertisement composition terminal market with the Linoscreen Composer, a device intended to compete with the Xenotron Video Composer (see 1977) *et al.*

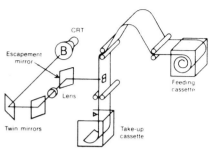

GSA 789

1980

J&P   Arthur Phillips had published a second major contribution to the literature of modern technology, namely a *Handbook of Computer-Aided Composition* (see 1968).

PTS   AM International sued the Itek Corporation for infringement of phototypesetting patents and gained quick reparation.

PTS   Rockwell International filed a suit against the Mergenthaler Linotype Co. complaining that the method of encoding outline digital founts for the Linotron 202, CRTronic, and Omnitech machines encroached upon the technology previously protected in the 'character generation method and systems' of the MGD Metro-Set phototypesetter. Early in 1983 an out-of-court settlement was sealed between the combatants. In 1984 the rights to the patent passed to Information International Inc.

PTS   H. Berthold AG secured control of Guttinger SA (see 1965), the Swiss manufacturer of a variety of front-end composition equipment as well as phototypesetting machines.

FES   Linotype Group of Companies absorbed Datek Systems Ltd.; the latter was a long-standing manufacturer of input and editing equipment.

FES   Linotype Group of Companies secured control of Mycro-Tek (see 1976), a short-lived corporate romance (see 1984).

PTS   Linotype and Morisawa established a joint-venture enterprise to develop and to market computer-based phototypesetting products in Japan and other areas using ideographic scripts.

FES   Norsk Data acquired Comtec, the long-standing Norwegian supplier of front-end composition systems.

FES   Penta Systems and Miles 33 ended their association and went separate ways (see 1976).

PTS   EditWriter II series of phototypesetters emerged using RAM-based logic. At the same time the maximum line length was stretched from 45 to 68 picas.

PTS Floppy disc module for capturing, storing, and retrieving keystrokes developed for the Quadritek 1200 direct-entry phototypesetter (see 1976).

PTS Several enhancements developed for the Linotron 202 (see 1978), instanced by a faster production rate of 800 lines per minute, by a refined vector outline program describing 'super founts', and by the integration of a rigid magnetic disc as an alternative to floppies for providing more capacious fount storage.

GRA Linotype Group of Companies unveiled a graphic sub-system for the Linotron 202. It consisted of an ECRM Autokon electronic camera for input scanning and a graphic screen for picture cropping and manipulation of tonal gradations.

PTS Compugraphic Corporation challenged for the middle ground of the digital CRT phototypesetting market by launching the CG 8600 machine. Nucleus of the system was twin Intel 8086 microprocessors with 32K (8-bit) RAM storage for digitised characters. Reserve founts were held on a sealed rigid disc of 14 to 28Mb. capacity. Founts were described in outline forms as straight-line vectors and a fibre-optic faceplate CRT served as the imaging vehicle at a resolution of 1,300 lines per inch.

PTS APSu5 digital CRT phototypesetter divulged by Autologic Inc. It jostled with the Linotron 202 and CG 8600 machines for industrial patronage. Founts were stored as run-length coding optionally on floppy, Winchester, or rigid magnetic discs. Microprocessor control was exercised by an Intel 8085 chip. Output speed was a phenomenal 1,250 lines per minute. Resolution varied on imaging from 602.5 to 2,410 lines per inch. Text generation occurred on a 5-inch CRT tube associated with enlarging optics.

PTS Xerox 5700 electronic printer heralded.

FES Hastech PagePro system was shown. It was designed primarily for the electronic assembly of newspaper pages.

1981

TYP Germany embodied the terms of the Vienna agreement on the protection of typefaces (see 1973) into its legal code.

TYP Herb Lubalin, the American graphic designer with many distinctions, died on 24 May. He was appointed Executive Vice-President of the International Typeface Corporation in 1971. His type designs include: Avant Garde Gothic (1970 with Tom Carnase), Serif Gothic (1974 with Antonio Di Spigna), and Lubalin Graph (1974 with Antonio Di Spigna and Joe Sundwall).

PTS Alphatype Corporation taken over by H. Berthold AG after protracted negotiations begun the previous year.

PTS Autologic Inc. purchased Bobst Graphic Systems.

FES Itek Corporation took over marketing of the Pagitek equipment developed by Heighlin Ltd. Pagitek was a very fast and endowed batch composition and pagination system.

FES Nearly $80,000,000 changed hands when Kodak purchased Atex Inc. It was not to be an isolated acquisition by the giant photographic supplier which seemed anxious to diversify, possibly haunted by several market forecasts projecting decline in the use of silver-based light sensitive materials.

TYP Bitstream Inc., a manufacturer of digital founts, formed by Mike Parker and Matthew Carter. Founts are provided as bit maps and in outline coding for a variety of low- and high-resolution imaging devices. First two customers were Camex and Scitex.

TYP Linotype Group of Companies contracted to supply the Xerox Corporation with specially-edited low-resolution digital founts for its electronic printers.

abcdefghijklmnopqrst
ABCDEFGHIJKLMNOPQ
1234567890 .,;:"«»&!?

Avante Garde Gothic

abcdefghijklmnopq
ABCDEFGHIJKLMNO
1234567890 .,;:"«»&!?

Lubalin Graph

FES   Raytheon Co. agreed to a takeover by Autologic Inc.

FES   Compugraphic Corporation diversified into newspaper composition front-end equipment with the acquisition of ONE Systems (see 1974).

PTS   Comp/Edit 5900 direct-entry phototypesetter revealed by AM International, a unit derived from the forerunning Comp/Edit 5810 (see 1978), but producing some three times faster at 75 characters per second. Increase in speed emanated from the application of a galvanometer mirror for escapement, instead of a stepping optical carriage characteristic of earlier machines in the series.

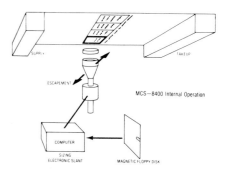

Schematic of MCS 8400

FES   Compugraphic Corporation launched the Modular Composition System (MCS) comprising video keyboards, various text storage units, controllers for clustering peripherals, and a couple of output phototypesetters. Numerous configurations of the modules could be determined to meet differing production requirements. Of the alternative phototypesetters, the MCS 8400 employed digital CRT imaging techniques, while the MCS 8200 adopted electro-mechanical photo-matrix methods.

PTS   Omnitech 2100 direct-entry phototypesetter announced; the machine exposed on to conventional silver-based light-sensitive materials as distinct from the zinc oxide paper applicable in the forerunning Omnitech 2000 (see 1979).

PTS   Dr. Boger organisation released the Scantext 1000 phototypesetter which wrote out the characters by a travelling CRT generating single scan lines consecutively in the manner of the Linotron 303 (see 1973). It was a brisk machine yielding 400 newspaper lines per minute, offering a type size range of 4 to 36 point, and providing retention of from 8 to 48 digital founts.

PTS   Compugraphic Corporation and the Itek Corporation embraced the CP/M operating system of personal computers into the MCS and Quadritek phototypesetting equipment respectively. Theoretically the development permitted the microprocessors embedded in the phototypesetters to run business and administrative software. In practice the benefits were largely illusory.

FES   IBM introduced its personal computer. Several systems integrators and software developers were to use the device as the kernel for composition systems.

FES   Movement towards electronic page make-up began to gain pace with several companies offering systems, such as Atex and Hastech.

FES   Xerox introduced the original Star 8010 video workstation. It revolutionised the man/machine interface through the use of icons, menus, and mouse control.

1982

MON   Monotype System 272 introduced for improving the efficiency of hot-metal composition by providing a video input keyboard coupled with facilities for editing and printing-out 31-channel spools.

TYP   Harry Carter, punchcutter, type designer, and typographic scholar, died on 10 March. His letter designs included a Baskerville Cyrillic for the Monotype Corporation.

PTS   Compugraphic Corporation, the market leader in the provision of phototypesetting equipment, was taken over by Agfa Gevaert.

FES   Harris Corporation acquired Logicon Inc., a supplier of front-end composition systems.

FES   Miles 33 (see 1980) became a public company.

FES   Royce Data Systems secured exclusive rights to the Imlac Composer (see 1971 and 1974).

FES   Xenotron Ltd. bought from AM International the text management interests of ECRM Inc. (see 1978).

TO   Society of Lithographic Artists, Designers, Engravers, and Process Workers (SLADE) merged with the National Graphical Association (NGA).

PTS   At DRUPA, Autologic/Bobst exhibited a couple of new second-generation phototypesetters, namely the APS-313 and APS-301. Only remarkable proposition was in the latter unit to expose characters on to zinc oxide paper and plate materials.

PTS   AM International released the Comp/Edit 6400, a machine with the same foreground facilities and characteristics as the Comp/Edit 5810 (see 1978), but equipped with a digital photo-unit. Founts were stored in Spirascan outline format founded on the digitising process developed by Peter Purdy and Ronald McIntosh. Generation of the characters for imaging occurred on a cathode ray tube at 1,300 lines per inch on the sensitive plane. Portions of a line up to 14 picas were generated on the tube; the images shone upwards to a mirror set at an angle of 45 degrees which in turn deflected them through a 2:1 reduction and escapement lens on to the film plane. When a section of the line had been completed, the lens escaped to the next exposure point and abbutted the succeeding section of text against that already exposed. In this manner a line of 70 picas could be readily assembled. Speed of the machine approximated to 90 characters per second.

PTS   Expansion occurred of the CRTronic direct-entry phototypesetter (see 1979) into three models 100, 150, and 200. Refinements related primarily to increased speed of output, to more capacious fount storage, and to a greater span of type sizes.

PTS   Multiple Application Phototypesetting System (MAPS) introduced by the Itek Corporation. It embraced up to four Quadritek Terminals on-line to a Media Unit comprising up to four floppy disc drives with a Quadritek 1400 or 1600 phototypesetter for output.

PTS   Additional improvements to the specification of the Linotron 202 phototypesetter (see 1978 and 1980) announced, including an extension of the longest line length to 70 picas, a higher output resolution of 1,950 lines per inch, and an increase in the largest type size to 96 point obtainable with 'super founts'.

PTS   Laserset phototypesetter appeared at DRUPA on the stand of Isys.

PTS   Scitex exhibited the Raystar flat-bed raster imaging phototypesetter.

FES   Linotype-Paul Ltd. introduced the APL-100 and APL-200 video input keyboards which incorporated Apple II personal computers. In the same year, Typecraft Systems Ltd. launched inexpensive terminals founded on the Commodore PET personal computer. Both developments were significant projects marking the beginning of a trend towards the use of less-specialised computer hardware produced in large volumes and at keen prices.

PTS   Agfa-Gevaert disclosed the P-400 electronic printer which originally imaged from a digital base with a laser and reproduced the results by electrophotographic techniques. Later linear LED (light emitting diode) arrays were substituted for the laser. Working to a resolution of 400 dots per inch and using a very effective dry toner, the P-400 printer ran at a speed of 18 pages per minute. Founts for the unit emanated from the Compugraphic Corporation.

PTS   IBM 4250 electro-erosion printer revealed at DRUPA. In effect, a moving head of 32 miniature electrodes was used to oxidise an aluminium foil, thereby uncovering an underlayer of black varnish which manifested the image. As a result of the process, a camera intermediate becomes available for copying. Resolution of the printer equates to 600 pixels per inch and production proceeds at a rate of an A4 page every 1.5 minutes. Typefaces for the printer had been licensed from a bunch of companies, including Monotype.

PTS   Xerox Corporation expanded its family of laser printers with the disclosure of the Xerox 2700 and Xerox 8700 machines: the units operated respectively at 12 and 80 pages per minute.

PTS   Xerox Corporation announced the availability of some Linotype founts for use on its electronic printers. It was salutary to see the results of expertly-edited typographic styles applied to laser printing at a resolution of 300 dots per inch.

FES   Autologic Inc. introduced the APS-Microcomposer multi-terminal typesetting system. Software was the work of European American Graphics which had Bob Shevlin as principal, an originator of the Varisystems Corporation.

FES   AM Varityper challenged for the multi-terminal composition system market with the release of Epics which envisaged a maximum configuration of eight workstations. Data storage on Winchester disc served as a shared resource, together with phototypesetters and proof printers.

FES   Bedford Computer Composition (see 1977) introduced a fresh composition system founded on an architecture of distributed processing and a local area network. Ethernet provided the means of integration with Meteor terminals as a prime component. Microprocessing was entrusted to Motorola 68000 chips with software written in the high-level C language running under the Unix operating system. Many other competitive configurations were destined to emerge containing similar characteristics.

FES   Penta Systems announced a new Pentavision terminal, a device intended to assist operator-intervention into the page make-up process as a support to a batch program. It incorporated the Motorola 68000 microprocessor with software written in the C language.

FES   Berthold tentatively revealed at DRUPA the Magic page assembly system which encompassed various components for manipulating interactively text and graphics and for merging them in output documents. Equipment included graphic screens, raster imaging typesetters, and input digitising scanners.

FES   Sim-X flaunted a raster image processor for displaying true typefaces on an interactive page make-up video screen and for driving low-resolution proof printers and high-resolution phototypesetters. In the latter category came the Sim-X Pagescan which utilised the imaging engine of the Lasercomp (see 1976).

FES   Xenotron Ltd. unveiled the PageMaster video make-up terminal.

FES   Corporate technical documentation was attracting increased attention as a potential market for composition equipment. Xyvision Inc. was established to cater for the anticipated demand. Its system was founded upon a network structure and encompassed terminals for text capure and editing, as well as a bit-map screen displaying a graphic simulation of the finished page. Strong batch pagination was another feature. Integration of text and graphics was a fundamental proposition. Eventually input scanners and imagesetters were interfaced to the system to keep faith with the original philosophy. Electronic printers constituted the means of proofing.

FES   Texet Corporation launched as a supplier of technical documentation systems. It shared a philosophy similar to Xyvision Inc., a fact reflected in the hardware and software engineering. Differences in emphasis and implementation existed, but the now obligatory bit-mapped WYSIWYG display was central to the configuration.

GRA   Imagitex inaugurated as a supplier of systems for handling digitised monochrome graphics. Equipment configurations consisted of a CCD input scanner for digitising illustrations, a storage module forming a graphics data base, an Imagitiser graphics screen for manipulating the scanned picture data, and later a raster image processor materialised. Imagitex equipment has tended to be promoted as a graphics sub-system for interfacing to other text composition and page make-up configurations.

PTS   Eocom disclosed plans for developing a raster image processor (RIP) to drive a laser platemaker.

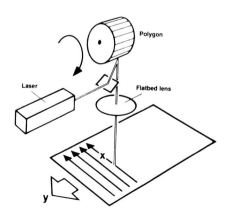

Eocom laser platemaking system

1983

PTS   Rene A. Higonnet, joint inventor of the Photon/Lumitype phototypesetting system, died on 14 October.

GRA AM International divested ECRM Inc. It was a short and barren liaison of scarcely five years' duration. ECRM was now free to concentrate on development of the line of Autokon electronic cameras, the original OCR scanning interest having been sold to Lundy Electronics and the text management systems to Xenotron Ltd.

PTS Kodak accelerated its acquisition and diversification programme by purchasing the ink jet printing interests of the Mead Corporation and by obtaining floppy disc manufacturing technology from Drivetec.

PTS Linotype-Paul Ltd. was pruned back by the corporate decision to concentrate manufacturing for the group in Germany and to conduct research and development in Germany and the USA only. As a consequence, Linotype-Paul was reduced to a sales and service organisation.

PTS Litton Industries acquired the Itek Corporation, but with little conviction for the graphic arts activities.

OCR OCR business of ECRM Inc. purchased by Lundy Electronics.

FES Schism occurred in Computer Composition Inc. with the American and European sections moving in different directions: the former portion being acquired by PSS Peripherals.

TO Under the new industrial legislation, Eddy Shah, Chairman of the Messenger Group of Newspapers in Warrington, challenged the validity of the closed shop by engaging non-union production workers. It was an important event that unsettled traditional labour practices of the industry.

PTS AM Varityper disclosed the Comp/Edit 6300, a machine identical in almost every respect to the preceding Comp/Edit 6400 (see 1982), except that a smaller video editing screen was incorporated which lessened the price of the unit and precluded access to digital preview facilities.

PTS Linotype Group of Companies introduced the Linotron 101, a raster imaging phototypesetter using a helium-neon laser deflected by an oscillating mirror to synthesise pages of text. Founts were stored digitally as outline coding.

PTS Itek Corporation released the Digitek phototypesetter. It employed an array of light-emitting diodes (LED), coupled to a fibre-optics bundle, for constructing images on red-sensitive paper. Seemingly the LED array, consisting of 128 light elements, travelled across the sensitive plane. The optical fibres gave a spot size of 0.002 inch diameter and made near-contact exposures on the paper. Output resolutions reached 667 and 1,333 lines per inch which yielded running speeds respectively of 80 and 45 characters per second.

FES PowerPage software packet released for the Modular Composition System by the Compugraphic Corporation.

PTS Autologic Inc. divulged a graphics converter interface (GCI) for its APS-5 and APSu5 phototypesetters.

PTS Compugraphic Corporation uncovered a graphics version of the MCS 8600 cathode ray tube phototypesetter. Text was imaged in the conventional manner by the machine, but graphics were output in a raster mode.

PTS Lasercomp Sprint divulged; the machine employed founts encoded as vectored outlines and embodied logic for dynamically sizing characters on the fly. Previous Lasercomp units operated with rasterised founts which had to be pre-sized in advance of running a job (see 1985: the Lasercomp Blaser).

PTS Compugraphic Corporation announced the Personal Composition System comprising an Apple Lisa computer with typesetting software driving MCS phototypesetters. Central to the philosophy was the integration of computer graphics and text.

PTS Canon LBP-CX electronic printer introduced with a rated speed of 8 pages per minute, a resolution of 300 dots per inch, a laser diode for imaging, a table-top design, and a readily-replaceable cartridge for consumables (e.g. toner).

FES   CText introduced a composition system based on IBM personal computers. Most notable was the networking of the workstations using 3Com Ethernet during 1984.

FES   PagePlanner system of composition and page assembly on a personal computer was divulged. Construction of pages depended upon the establishment of an 'electronic' layout into which text was allowed to flow. PagePlanner did much to fashion market expectations of systems founded on personal computer hardware.

PTS   Scangraphic Dr. Boger announced the Graphic Page terminal for the Scantext phototypesetting system: a preview screen showing true type styles and sizes.

FES   Harris 8300 page make-up workstation exhibited. It had some philosophical similarities to the Hastech PagePro (see 1980).

FES   Interleaf joined the growing ranks of suppliers attempting to serve the corporate technical documentation market.

FES   Intran harnessed the Perq workstation for the composition of pages incorporating text and graphics. Target market for the system was electronic printing, particularly users of Xerox machines.

FES   Proliferation continued of companies intent on serving the in-plant technical documentation market. Qubix, Viewtech, and Caddex threw hats in the ring during the year. Text and graphics integration into page form was the declared objective using the bit-mapped display as an essential tool for image simulation electronically.

FES   System Integrators Inc., a supplier of multi-terminal composition systems, commenced marketing in Europe.

FES   Camex Inc. unveiled a new range of products planned around a raster image processor known as the BitCaster. It was used to create the images displayed on a Breeze make-up terminal, as well as to drive the BitSetter 3100 and the BitPrinter machines. The BitSetter was a high-resolution 1,000-lines-per-inch phototypesetter founded on the Lasercomp imaging engine, while the BitPrinter utilised a low-resolution 240 dots per inch Canon copier engine. The Breeze terminal displayed true founts. Overall the Camex SuperSetter system heralded a fresh generation of products.

FES   Adobe Systems released details of a powerful raster image processor and a page descriptor software package called PostScript. The latter was designed to accept text and graphics according to pre-arranged conventions for input to the raster image processor which generated a corresponding raster data stream.

FES   Autologic Inc. disclosed the Bit Blaster raster image processor for proofing APS-5 and APSu5 output on a Xerox XP-12 laser printer.

PTS   Pilot installation of a direct computer-to-plate system installed at the *Utica Observer* in the state of New York. Hastech provided the page make-up facilities complementing the Eocom raster image processor and laser platemaker (see 1982). The project did not succeed and was subsequently discontinued.

GRA   Logotype sub-system disclosed by Scangraphic Dr. Boger for the Scantext phototypesetting system consisting of a small drum scanner for input and character editing software to run on a standard terminal. To aid clean up of the scanned characters, a Digipen was also released.

1984

LIN   Linotype & Machinery Ltd. purchased the residual hot-metal business of Harris Graphics Ltd. Implicit in the agreement was the manufacture of linecasting machines, spare parts, and matrices.

TF   Ludwig & Mayer GmbH, the typefoundry, closed.

PTS   Compugraphic Corporation established a subsidiary company in the United Kingdom by acquiring the distributorship of M. H. Whittaker & Son Ltd.

FES   Linotype Group of Companies divested Mycro-Tek as part of a broader rationalisation programme.

FES   Unitex was formed as a reincarnation of the Itek Large Systems Operations. Such an evolution was a direct consequence of the acquisition of the Itek Corporation by Litton Industries (see 1983). Products devolving to the new company were notably the Copy Processing Systems of considerable longevity and traceable to Xylogics Inc. (see 1971).

PTS   AM Varityper instituted the Advanced Imaging Software on Comp/ Edit CRT phototypesetters. It offered reverse video facilities and near interactivity on the digital preview screen.

FES   Compugraphic Corporation expanded the Modular Composition System by an MCS 100 controller capable of supporting up to eight terminals. In addition, the controller could serve up to a pair of phototypesetters and a couple of preview electronic proofing screens. Storage modules in the forms of Winchester discs with greater capacities were also embraced (see 1981).

GRA   Compugraphic Corporation brought out a system for processing digital monochrome graphics, both line and halftone. It involved application of an intelligent Scanner 2000; the MCS 8600 Imagesetter (see 1983) with a higher resolution for graphics of 1,156 dots per inch as opposed to the earlier 578; and the PowerPage software running on an MCS controller for positioning elements in a page by encoding co-ordinate positions. Note the storage of digital graphics was not practised.

PTS   Scangraphic Dr. Boger enhanced the range of Scantext equipment with Supertype founts for outputting sizes up to 360 point.

PTS   Alphatype CRS 9900 digital CRT phototypesetter introduced. It had a moderate running speed of 600,000 characters per hour.

PTS   Linotype Group of Companies released the Linotronic 300 phototypesetter, a raster scan imaging device employing a spinning polygon mirror for deflecting a helium-neon laser beam across a page. Finest resolution attainable was 2,540 lines per inch, though coarser scans could be summoned. Special laser founts were developed for the machine encoded in outline form as straight lines and arcs.

PTS   Dr.-Ing. Rudolf Hell revealed the LS210 typesetter, a device combining a raster image processor with a flat-bed laser recorder.

PTS   Ricoh 4080 electronic printer announced, an active competitor to the Canon LBP-CX (see 1983).

GRA   Monotype International unveiled a graphics sub-system for the Lasercomp. It encompassed an input digitising scanner (e.g. ECRM Autokon or Imagitex), a file manager and database, and a graphics screen for cropping and tonally adjusting pictures.

PTS   Tegra promoted the Genesis electronic printer as a plain paper typesetter. It flaunted a resolution of a little over 500 dots per inch vertically and 1,000 dots per inch horizontally which constituted a marked contrast with the forerunning coarser-resolution electronic printers. Speed was quoted at 1,500 lines per minute. Considerable typographical flexibility was incorporated in the machine derived from its raster image processor.

PTS   Monotype International demonstrated the Lasercomp raster image processor driving low-resolution laser printers for the purposes of plain paper proofing, such as the Xerox 2700 and the Canon LBP-10.

FES   Bestinfo offered a composition program (Type Processor One) running on an IBM personal computer with provision for WYSIWYG viewing on a screen.

FES   Compugraphic Corporation divulged the PowerView 10 terminal. It used a split screen. One area offered an electronic representation of the job as composing proceeded, while the other area displayed source code with embedded functions which could be changed to reflect in the representation display. Floppy discs were employed for text storage.

FES   Linoscreen Composer 2 announced. It embodied a number of improvements over the original model (see 1979), such as greater processing speed, increased fount storage, and larger screen buffer.

FES   Atex and Camex reached a joint agreement whereby the former company would integrate into its composition systems the Breeze terminal and the SuperSetter products of the latter organisation.

FES   IBM broke cover with the Document Composition Facility designed to assemble pages of integrated text and graphics for output imaging by the IBM 4250 electro-erosion printer (see 1982).

FES   Interset announced the low-cost Protext 1000 composition system and a mathematics software packet for the more endowed Protext 2000 configuration.

FES   Miles 33 unveiled the Magpie graphic workstation for designing and assembling pages. Additionally the Miles composition systems had graduated to a local area network complete with microprocessor-based terminals. Several other components had been integrated, such as a Xerox 2700 laser printer for proofing and an Imagitex sub-system for graphics handling.

FES   Royce Data Systems announced a composition configuration aimed at the in-plant technical documentation market. It had the imperative WYSIWYG video screen and the Motorola 68000 chip for data processing.

FES   Scangraphic Dr. Boger released the Scandata 100 Data Management System with provision for clusters of up to four terminals plus output devices.

FES   System Integrators Inc. announced a new classified pagination and advertisement dummying software package for its systems.

FES   Viewtech (see 1983) issued more details of its new composition system. It espoused the concept of conducting text and graphics manipulation on a single WYSIWYG terminal which was felt to be sympathetic to the needs of document creators (i.e. writers and illustrators). Some other systems tended to favour a variety of specialised terminals for different purposes integrated over a network.

FES   Xerox Publishing System 700 released. It involved the now normal ingredients of an in-plant documentation system, such as a batch-processing composition program, a bit-mapped WYSIWYG display, a felicitous and graphic man/machine interface, and a series of low-level entry terminals based on personal computer hardware (Xerox 820).

FES   Xyvision Inc. commenced marketing in Europe under the experienced and knowledgeable leadership of Brian Mulholland.

GRA   ECRM Inc. announced the Autokon 1000 monochrome laser scanner.

PTS   Lasercomp used for exposing directly on to the Agfa SetPrint paper printing plate.

PTS   Chelgraph Ltd. formed by Derek Kyte and partners to develop advanced composition products, such as raster image processors, composition software for personal computers, WYSIWYG displays, and output image recorders.

PTS   Verbal Technologies Inc. exhibited the Text Talking Terminal. The unit was founded on an IBM personal computer complete with a voice synthesiser which received coded text files from a front-end composition system and enunciated the contents. The proofreader checked the oral rendering of the captured text against the copy, a reversal of the usual process.

1985

TYP   Hans Schmoller died on 25 September. He joined Penguin Books as the successor to Jan Tschichold (see 1974) in 1949 and retired in 1976. Much of the reputation of the publisher for stylish and expertly designed books is attributable to him. His standards of graphic design, typography, and composition were uncompromising. From 1947 to 1949, Schmoller worked for the Curwen Press in London.

PTS   Klaus Paul, founder of K. S. Paul Ltd., died on 6 December. He was a far-sighted and patient financial backer of the PM 1001 phototypesetter which eventually became the Linotron 505 (see 1967).

TYP Herbert Bayer, a graphic designer and teacher at the Bauhaus School, died on 30 September (see 1925).

FES Intran (see 1983) filed for Chapter XI under the USA bankruptcy laws, as did Viewtech. Both companies had been established to exploit the corporate technical publishing market.

PTS Linotype-Paul Ltd. became simply Linotype Ltd.

PTS Litton Industries elected to sell Itek Graphic Systems.

TF Mergenthaler Linotype GmbH attained sole ownership of the typefounders Stempel AG. Previously the level of shareholding had been 60 per cent for some 80 years. The foundry was soon closed

TO *Express & Star* of Wolverhampton became the second newspaper in Britain to adopt single keyboarding procedures whereby journalists input copy directly to a composition computer through video terminals.

FES Use of personal computers for composition continued to gain pace: Interset took on the British distributorship for Bestinfo and Press Computer Systems did the same for CText.

FES Royce Data Systems acquired by Scitex.

FES Unitex (see 1984) entered receivership and was acquired by Chorus Data Systems; the trading names chosen for the new division were Cuneiform Systems in North America and Utex in Europe. Included in the equipment portfolio were the CPS and Minitek front-end systems, the Viewtex page dummying system, and the Mark IX cathode ray tube typesetter.

PTS Linotype Group of Companies disclosed a Series 100 system at PRINT 85. It consisted of an Apple Macintosh personal computer running Aldus PageMaker software: a combination with an effective man/machine interface and capable of assembling complete pages. Output devices comprised the Linotron 101 and the Apple LaserWriter printer operated through Apple and Adobe raster image processors. Workstations in the system could be integrated by the AppleTalk network. Later the Linotronic 100 substituted for the Linotron 101, while the Linotronic 300 constituted an alternative.

PTS AM Varityper introduced the Comp/Edit 6200 direct-entry digital phototypesetter. It was a scaled down version of the more endowed Comp/Edit 6400 (see 1982). Most notable difference was a small video screen of 14 lines, as opposed to 40 lines on the more venerable machine. Other specifications reflected a setting speed of 100 lines per minute, a type memory for up to eight styles, a line length of 48 picas, a type size range from 5 to 72 point, and a front end memory of 128K.

PTS Itek Corporation unveiled the Digitek 3000 direct-entry phototypesetter, an upgraded version of the LED imaging unit dating from 1983 (q.v.). The newer model had much greater flexibility, notably in the ability to size dynamically and to slant, condense, and expand electronically digital fount masters. Point size range extended from 5 to 72 point. Up to 16 type styles were resident in the floppy disc configuration and more than 250 in the Winchester disc version.

PTS Compugraphic Corporation uncovered the MCS 8000 digital CRT phototypesetter. It was a derivative of the MCS 8400 (see 1981) and cheaper. Two versions of the MCS 8000 eventually appeared operating respectively at 100 and 50 lines per minute. Output resolution equalled 2,600 lines per inch. Some 10 to 12 type styles were resident reproducible over a range from 5 to 72 point. Widest line length was 70 picas. Special and proprietary ZMR paper and film had to be used.

PTS Another version of the MCS 8000 phototypesetter surfaced in the autumn. Unlike previous models of the machine which incorporated floppy disc drives for the local storage of founts, the new unit relied upon an MCS controller to download the type styles into an area of RAM.

PTS   Linotype Group of Companies rationalised the CRTronic phototypesetter family with the models 320, 340, and 360. Differences related principally to output speeds and to image resolutions.

PTS   Compugraphic Corporation added a mathematics software and typographic package to the Modular Composition System.

PTS   Refined digital founts were issued by the Compugraphic Corporation for the MCS 8400 cathode ray tube phototypesetter. They were encoded in outline, but contained a greater number of shorter vectors than previous founts. Type Plus was the trade name adopted.

PTS   Digitek 3000 phototypesetter from the Itek Corporation was endowed with a ruling software package and an electronic proofing preview screen displaying true type styles and sizes at a resolution of 105 dots per inch.

GRA   Compugraphic Corporation launched the Scanner 1000, together with an IBM personal computer for accepting and for pixel editing the scanned graphics data. Primary purpose of the sub-system was to provide logotypes for the MCS 8400 digital phototypesetter. The Scanner 1000 was a desk-top unit and operated as a flat-bed CCD device. Resolution of scanner input was 203 dots per inch, as opposed to output on the MCS 8400 at 578 dots per inch.

GRA   Logotype sub-system consisting of a Datacopy input scanner, an IBM personal computer, and character editing software introduced for the CRTronic, Linotron 202, and Linotronic 300 machines.

PTS   AM Varityper announced the Comp/Edit 6850 slave phototypesetter as an output device for front-end composition systems bearing the same brand name. It derived from the technology of the Comp/Edit 6400 (see 1982). Digital founts were encoded in outline as sections of a spiral curve. Image generation took place on a small cathode ray tube. Character escapement was a joint function of CRT spot deflection and of continuous movement of a lens. In effect, the lens travel simulated a raster scan motion. Typographic characters were exposed bidirectionally at speeds of up to 400 lines per minute, while the synthesis of line graphics occurred unidirectionally in swathes of image 14 points deep. Later in the year a couple of slower models were added to the product line: the Comp/Edit 6830 and Comp/Edit 6810. All founts were downloaded to the machines from a composition system.

PTS   AM International unveiled three slave phototypesetters: the Comp/Edit 6750, 6730, and 6710. Each machine had local storage for the handling of digital founts and was designed to be driven by the front-end composition systems of other manufacturers.

PTS   Alphatype CRS 4900 phototypesetter announced. It utilised a continuously-moving cathode ray tube to span measures up to 70 picas. Output resolution reached 5,300 lines per inch. Type size range extended from 5 to 72 point. Running speed was quoted as 150 lines per minute. For fount storage a Winchester disc of 40Mb. capacity was employed.

GRA   Agreement reached whereby the Linotype Group of Companies would integrate into its text composition configurations the graphics sub-systems of Imagitex (see 1982). Output recording of text and graphics was done on the Linotronic 300.

PTS   ECRM Inc. divulged the PelBox, the output recording portion of the Autokon 1000 laser scanner (see 1984). Output resolution was 1,016 lines per inch writing at a speed of 5 inches per minute over a 12-inch line length. Naturally a raster image processor would be necessary to operate the unit, probably provided by the vendor of the front-end composition system.

PTS   Reincarnation of the Linotron 101 (see 1983) occurred with emergence of the Linotronic 100, a machine embodying a sturdier galvanometer mirror action, an output media cassette inherited from the Linotron 202, and a power supply derived from the CRTronic.

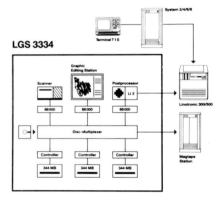

LGS 3334

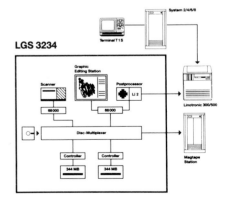

LGS 3234

Linotype graphic sub-systems

PTS Monotype International released the Lasercomp Blaser, a reincarnation of the lapsed Lasercomp Sprint. The new machine had a rated speed of 16 inches per minute.

PTS Improvements to the Linotronic 300 took place in the form of faster recording by more than two-fold and in the ability to generate tints and patterns.

PTS Xenotron Ltd. unveiled the UX Imagesetter, a raster imaging recorder using a diode laser as the light source. Maximum resolution of output was stated as 2,400 dots per inch, though others obtainable equalled 1,200, 800, 600, 480, 300, and 240. The media was stepped by a motor, rather than driven continuously as on alternative devices. As a consequence, the recording process could be stopped at any time to allow associated functions to keep pace. Speed of recording reached 8.5 inches per minute at a resolution of 1,200 dots per inch. Laser beam deflection derived from two facets of a spinning optical pyramid. To drive the machine, Xenotron provided a raster image processor, but OEM versions of the recorder only were available to other manufacturers.

PTS Data Recording Systems launched the LaserScribe 8415 electronic printer. Output resolution was 400 or 800 dots per inch, though models offering 600 and 1,000 dots per inch have been predicted. Rate of production was quoted as slightly under four A4 pages per minute at 800 dots per inch.

PTS IBM 3820 electronic printer released. Specifications encompassed a speed of 20 pages per minute, a resolution of 240 dots per inch, an ability to perfect sheets, and an internal raster image processor.

PTS Xerox 3700 laser printer divulged, a machine operating at 24 pages per minute and perpetuating the resolution of 300 dots per inch practised by other machines in the family.

FES Bestinfo presaged the merging of text and graphics through the use of a microcomputer at the PRINT 85 exhibition in Chicago. The system was based on an IBM personal computer running the SuperPage software package and incorporating a WYSIWYG screen. Digital graphics were captured and input by means of a Datacopy 700 CCD flat-bed scanner (see 1984).

FES IBM personal computers with text-editing software interfaced to the Alphatype Multi-Set system.

FES Itek Corporation introduced a Personal Typesetting Workstation. It comprised an IBM personal computer running a composition program developed by Chelgraph Ltd. (see 1984). Central to the system was a WYSIWYG display.

FES Linotype Group of Companies gained some distribution rights to the PagePlanner (see 1983) software running on an IBM personal computer to drive the Linotronic 100 and Linotron 202 phototypesetters. Additionally a second package of input and editing software, for operating on the same PC hardware, was obtained, namely the Microsoft Word.

FES AM Varityper released a new version of the Epics text management system using hardware based on the Motorola 68000 processor, instead of the Zilog Z80 and Z8000 chips as formerly. Software improvements covered vertical justification, automatic footnote placement, stronger protection against widow lines in pagination, and so on.

FES Autologic Inc. announced the Microcomposer II front-end system, a faster and more capable version of a previously available product.

FES Compugraphic Corporation introduced several improvements to the PowerView 10 terminal: (1) a Winchester disc drive was added to store programs, founts, and data; (2) a couple of PowerView 10 terminals could be configured to share a database by means of an Ethernet interface; and (3) a PowerView 10 terminal could be linked to an MCS 10 or MCS 100 controller to access data files on their floppy or hard discs.

FES   System Integrators Inc. divulged System/25 based on local area network architecture and distributed processing. Primary target market was small- and medium-scale newspapers.

FES   AM Varityper offered a preview of the Graphics Text Organiser (GTO) Terminal. It was based on Perq hardware and functioned as an interactive page layout and make-up system. Text was flowed into an established page geometry. True type styles and sizes were displayed on the bit-mapped screen.

PTS   Autologic Inc. released a range of raster image processors with differing capabilities of speed, resolution, and typographical and graphical flexibility. Additionally the company announced several complementary output recorders, namely: the APS-6 80/Laser, the APS-6 70/CRT, and the APS-6 108/CRT. Raster resolution varied from 723 to 1,446 lines per inch. Speed of the laser recorder was quoted as 15 inches per minute at a resolution of 1,000 lines per inch, whereas the CRT recorders ran faster at 24 inches per minute in a comparable resolution. Bidco was the originator of the helium-neon laser recording engine.

FES   Apple Computer disclosed the AppleTalk local area network, the Apple LaserWriter electronic printer, and transformed the Apple Lisa 2/10 computer into the Apple Macintosh XL. By a licensing agreement, Linotype founts were provided for the Apple LaserWriter printer.

FES   Linotype Group of Companies concluded a number of significant agreements. Firstly a decision to supply type founts for the Apple LaserWriter electronic printer, a device that could serve for proofing, for sub-master making, and for short-run demand printing within the context of Linotype systems. Secondly an accord was reached with Adobe Systems for the use of a raster image processor to drive the Linotronic 100 and Linotronic 300 phototypesetters. Thirdly an agreement was made to employ the Apple Macintosh computer, running PageMaker software from the Aldus Corporation, for output to the two Linotronic machines.

1986

SO   Manufacture of type founts for Varityper strike-on machines discontinued (see 1978).

PTS   The Monotype Corporation Ltd. regained the status of a public company with a quotation on the Unlisted Securities Market.

PTS   Management buyout of the Itek Graphic and Composition Divisions occurred. To reflect new ownership, the company adopted the name Itek Graphix Corporation.

GRA   DuPont bought a 12 per cent stake in Imagitex (see 1982), a developer and supplier of digital monochrome graphics systems.

TYP   Esselte Letraset acquired the International Typeface Corporation.

TYP   Digital Type Systems Ltd. established as a supplier of digital type founts by Robert Norton, Bill Wheatley, and Ernst Imhoff.

PTS   Compugraphic Corporation agreed to pay $5,000,000 to Information International Inc. in respect of alleged infringement of the patent covering the outline coding of digital founts (see 1980).

FES   Crosfield Electronics Ltd. acquired Hastech, the supplier of front-end composition systems. Hastech was an outgrowth from Hendrix Electronics Inc., an early exponent of video text editing in the graphic arts (see 1969 and 1970). It is somewhat ironical that Crosfield became a British distributor for Hendrix equipment in 1970.

FES   The Monotype Corporation obtained a 75 per cent shareholding in GB techniques.

FES   Xyvision Inc. agreed to develop a networked workstation and file server for the Linotype Group of Companies.

FES   Viewtech (see 1983 and 1984), a supplier of an in-plant technical documentation system, emerged from Chapter XI of the USA bankruptcy laws.

FES   A. B. Dick Co. established an Electronic Publishing Division.

GRA   Muirhead Data Communications purchased by Crosfield Electronics Ltd. Included in the Muirhead product portfolio were facsimile flat-bed scanners and recorders and the electronic picture desk for newspapers.

FES   Xenotron Ltd. acquired by the Hell organisation in Germany.

FES   Voracious mood of Crosfield Electronics continued with the take over of Composition Systems Inc. (see 1967).

FES   Cuneiform Systems (see 1985) ceased trading. Rights to the CPS Front-End Composition System passed to Computer Peripheral Sciences.

PTS   H. Berthold AG sold 51 per cent of its interest in the Alphatype Corporation to Klaus Busch, a move taken in the wake of reported heavy financial losses by the German machinery manufacturer.

TO   News International, publishers of *The Times* and *Sun* newspapers in London, began printing at a new plant in Wapping. Production was handled by workers in membership of the Electrical, Electronic, Telecommunications, and Plumbing Union, instead of by the established print unions of the National Graphical Association and the Society of Graphical and Allied Trades 82. It was a landmark event involving new technology which altered entrenched trade attitudes and served as a catalyst for broader changes in Fleet Street.

PTS   Linotype Group of Companies disclosed the Linotronic 500, a wide-measure version of the Linotronic 300 (see 1984) laser typesetter. It encompassed measures up to 108 picas. Three output resolutions and speeds were obtainable on the machine: 1,690 lines per inch at 6 inches per minute; 845 lines per inch at 22 inches per minute; and 420 lines per inch at 40 inches per minute. Up to 1,000 type styles could be stored on a 20Mb. Winchester disc, while the type size range spanned from 4 to 186 point. Photographic positives and negatives could be produced by the machine, both right- and wrong-reading.

PTS   Monotype International disclosed the Lasercomp Pioneer. Two output resolution/speed combinations were accessible on the equipment, namely: 1,000 lines per inch at 18 inches per minute and 1,500 lines per inch at 10 inches per minute.

PTS   Monotype 512 direct-entry phototypesetter unveiled at DRUPA. It embodied a unique imaging technology based on a light-switching array (LiSA) chip developed by Philips. In essence the chip had 512 potential exposure points which could be made transparent or opaque by the drive circuitry. Behind the chip was a light source. Images were synthesised by traversing the chip in front of the photo-sensitive material, thereby generating a pseudo raster scan. Output resolution was 1,000 dots per inch. Speed attained 80 characters per second. Type size range stretched from 5.5 to 72 point in quarter-point steps. Up to 1,000 type styles could be accommodated on-line. Front-end logic for text entry, editing, and composition was in the form of an Olivetti M24 personal computer. Output materials were orthochromatic.

PTS   Itek Graphix Corporation introduced the Digitek 5000 phototypesetter, an improved version of the Model 3000 (see 1985). Its 'print' head was still based on LED imaging, but dispensed with the need for fibre optics to convey the light to the sensitive plane.

PTS   Yet another model added to the Lasercomp family of machines by Monotype International, namely the Lasercomp Express. It was said to produce broadsheet newspaper pages at a rate of one per minute and at a resolution of 1,000 lines per inch. Dual processing was practised at the front-end which permitted a page to be imaged simultaneously with image processing (i.e. bit map preparation) of the next.

PTS   Compugraphic Corporation entered the growing world of lasersetting by release of the CG9600. It employed a helium-neon laser deflected by a holographic spinner for composing an image. Speed and

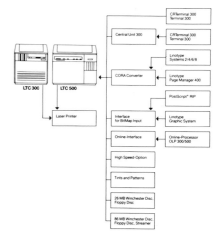

Linotronic 300 & 500 system

resolution ratings were 10 inches per minute at 1,200 dots per inch and 4.5 inches per minute at 2,400 dots per inch. Maximum line length reached 78 picas. Type sizes ranged from 4 to 999 point. Founts were encoded as outlines and in a new 'curvilinear' format which maintained the integrity of character shapes, notably on the curves. Two 10Mb. Winchester discs constituted part of the standard configuration. One served to store founts and graphics and the other to store programs and page bit maps ready for imaging. Electronic modulation of type characters was enabled by logic, such as slanting, condensing, and expanding. Graphics were fully supported by the CG9600, including the imaging of halftones. Driving the machine was a Compugraphic raster image processor founded on the Intel 80186 microprocessor.

PTS   Berthold Laser Station shown at DRUPA. It comprised a Chelgraph raster image processor driving an ECRM PelBox laser recorder. Output resolution was 2,000 dots per inch. Additionally the raster image processor could control a Canon CX printer for the purposes of plain paper proofing. For storing founts, a personal computer completed the configuration.

PTS   Berthold HR Recorder uncovered at DRUPA. Components consisted of a Berthold raster image processor and a CRT imaging engine. Built around a Motorola 68020 microprocessor, the RIP incorporated 6Mb. of RAM and a 70Mb. Winchester disc; while the output recorder comprised a small CRT that moved along a carriageway in front of the photo-sensitive material. Each traverse of the CRT fashioned some 500 to 730 scan lines. Focusing lens and deflecting mirror completed the optics. Resolutions on output were alternatively 3,550 or 1,775 dots per inch. Recording speeds were 12 inches and 7 inches per minute depending on the resolution.

PTS   ECRM introduced a model of the PelBox (see 1985) laser image recorder covering a maximum line length of 108 picas, instead of a previous 72 picas. Resolution remained at 1,016 dots per inch, but the speed more than doubled to 11.5 inches per minute.

PTS   Several enhancements were made by Scangraphic Dr. Boger to the Scantext 1000 system, such as the integration of personal computers for text input and editing, the development of a multi-disc reader for capturing data from external devices, and the provision of plain paper proofing on a Canon print engine driven by a proprietary Scangraphic raster image processor.

PTS   Scangraphic Dr. Boger announced the Scantext 2000 system for processing text and graphics. New units embraced by the developments were: (1) a Commander workstation for combining text and graphics into page form, (2) an intelligent flat-bed CCD image scanner 1015, and (3) a couple of laser typesetters labelled respectively 2030 and 2051. The Commander workstation was founded on Motorola 68000 microprocessors and embodied a 15-inch diagonal high-resolution screen displaying 256 grey levels. Its resolution was 108 lines per inch. System memory was expandable to 6Mb. supplemented by Winchester discs of varying capacities up to 72Mb. Floppy discs were incorporated in the configuration. User interface encompassed a mouse, tablet, stylus, keyboard, and WYSIWYG screen. The 1015 image scanner was of CCD flat-bed construction and accepted line, halftone, and continuous-tone subjects. Originals up to 10 x 15 inches could be handled. Characteristics of the laser typesetters were line lengths of 70 picas (model 2030) and 120 picas (model 2051), together with resolutions of 812, 1,625, and 3,251 lines per inch. Laserproof 1000 was another element in the Scantext 2000 system for plain paper proofing.

PTS   At DRUPA, Chelgraph Ltd. (see 1984) exhibited the IBX typesetter. It employed a fibre-optic faceplate CRT for exposing scan lines horizontally across the photo-sensitive medium at a density of 1,000 dots per inch and at a speed of 15 inches per minute. Controlling the machine was the Chelgraph RIP utilising founts Cambray-coded in outline and accepting data consistent with the conventions of the ACE command language. The IBX applied CRT technology in a novel manner which could potentially challenge the omnipresence of the laser in the area of raster imaging. Several companies elected to market the IBX image recorder on an OEM basis, as instanced by Alfa System Partner, Ferranti, Graphic Systems, and Monotype. Equally popular was the Chelgraph raster image processor which had been adopted by several machinery suppliers.

PTS Graphitel S.A. in France launched a new laser phototypesetter with Louis Moyroud as part of the design group. Called the Graphitel AC7020, the machine used a helium-neon laser as the light source deflected by a travelling mirror. In practice the laser beam was split into 256 sub-beams which resulted in exposing swathes of image about 16 points deep. Claimed speed was 1,000,000 characters per hour at a resolution of 1,156 dots per inch. About a dozen digitised type styles could be stored on a floppy disc or 200 on a Winchester disc. Point size range extended from 4.5 to 128. Founts were encoded in the Ikarus format. Maximum line length reached 108 picas.

PTS With 180 systems installed, Purup Electronics had become a major supplier of forms composition systems. At DRUPA the company exhibited higher-resolution laser image recorders up to 2,540 dots per inch which exposed at faster speeds than formerly: the polygon mirror spinning at 6,000 revolutions per minute compared to 3,000 revolutions per minute previously. On the new PE9000 recorder, the polygon ran at 12,000 revolutions per minute. Additionally the company showed a CCD input scanner for halftones with an array of 10,000 photosensors and digitising at 16 to 256 levels of grey scale. Less expensive workstations (e.g. PE1600) based on the Motorola 68020 chip were also divulged. In keeping with the craze of the day, an interface for personal computers had been developed to allow the input of text.

PTS Laser printer plain paper proofing added to the facilities of the Linotronic 300 and 500 systems.

PTS Itek Graphix Corporation integrated a Canon LBP-CX print engine with a proprietary controller into the Digitek (see 1983 and 1985) product line for the purpose of plain paper proofing. The controller logic was derived essentially from the Digitek Preview terminal.

PTS AM Varityper launched the LP 2300 laser plain paper proofing system as an adjunct to a variety of its equipment, such as the Comp/Edit line of phototypesetters, the Epics text management system, and the Graphics Text Organiser (GTO) terminal.

PTS Itek Graphix Corporation provided electronic printer output for the Personal Typesetting Workstation (see 1985). Both the software for the terminal and the raster image processor and controller for the printer were developed by Chelgraph Ltd. (see 1984).

PTS Apple Computer announced availability of the LaserWriter Plus electronic printer and the Macintosh Plus microcomputer.

FES Terminal 300 released by the Linotype Group of Companies: a lower-cost version of the CR Terminal. It incorporated a single floppy disc drive only and a somewhat smaller keyboard.

FES Compugraphic Corporation released a PowerView 5 workstation. It was a direct derivative of the PowerView 10 terminal (see 1984) and adopted the same philosophy of a split screen to display simultaneously the source coding, together with an electronic simulation of the appearance of the finished job. PowerView 5 encompassed a 12-inch diagonal screen with a landscape aspect, as opposed to the PowerView 10 with a 15-inch diagonal screen of portrait aspect.

FES Personal computers integrated into the MCS system by the Compugraphic Corporation. Labelled the Personal Typography System, the software ran on IBM hardware with 256K main memory and dual floppy disc drives. As an option, a Winchester disc can be substituted for one of the floppies.

FES   IBM introduced the RT PC workstation.

GRA   DuPont announced development of a monochrome digital graphics system based on the Imagitex equipment. At the same time a deal was struck with the Linotype Group of Companies for the provision of Linotronic 300 machines to serve as high-resolution output recorders for the projected configuration.

FES   Central Unit 300 launched by the Linotype Group of Companies. It afforded the means for the on-line integration of CRTronic and Linotronic products and for providing a shared data base to the connected equipment. Two Motorola 68000 microprocessors were contained in the unit, together with a Winchester disc of 20Mb. or 67Mb. formatted capacity. Up to a dozen input stations (e.g. CRTerminal) could be supported along with four output units (e.g. CRTronic 360, Linotronic 100, Linotronic 300).

FES   Compugraphic Corporation moved strongly towards the implementation of a local area network to integrate its disparate products; the Ethernet interface and protocol served as the adopted vehicle. Supported on the Ethernet were personal computers (the PTS Composer), PowerView 5 and 10 workstations, and MCS 10 and 100 controllers. Up to eight individual workstations could be accommodated on the network, but should one of the nodes be occupied by an MCS 100 controller with eight terminals, the total number of users would climb to fifteen.

FES   Networking of up to sixteen of the Harris 8300 (see 1983) page layout terminals was introduced.

FES   CCI (see 1974 and 1976) in Europe converted to NCR host computers for its composition systems. Also a Champion workstation with an interactive WYSIWYG screen was added to the product portfolio. Hardware for the new terminal was from Sun Microsystems complete with Motorola 68020 chip. System memory was 4Mb. supported by a 71Mb. Winchester disc. Graphics entered the system from Microtek and Autokon scanners. For output CCI employed the Xenotron UX Imagesetter (see 1975).

FES   ONE Systems incorporated personal computers into its front-end composition systems. Additionally the product name was changed to Intrepid and extends to three models: the Intrepid 18, 32, and 48. Mercifully the figures do have significance and denote the maximum numbers of terminals supported (see 1974 and 1981).

FES   Interset previewed at DRUPA a high-resolution WYSIWYG display terminal based on the Motorola 68020 processor. It served as a peripheral to the established Protext system (see 1984).

FES   Mycro-Tek provided a driver program for the LaserWriter electronic printer. It enabled Mycro-Comp 1100-Plus and 550 composition systems to offer plain paper proofing facilities. At the same time, the company integrated personal computers into its configurations as an alternative to specialised terminals for the inputting and editing of text.

FES   Xyvision Inc. introduced layout-driven software for the production of magazine pages on its Xyview workstations. In essence a page could be defined electronically on the screen and typographical attributes established in readiness for the text to be allowed to flow into the individual areas. Afterwards the various elements could be re-arranged on the screen interactively. It marked a significant development, as previously Xyvision had concentrated on batch pagination of fairly standard documents and allowed human interaction at a WYSIWYG screen to repair 'batch' errors.

GRA   Line graphics and logotype sub-system developed for the Digitek phototypesetter (see 1983 and 1985). It comprised a 300 dots-per-inch Ricoh input image scanner and bit map editing software for implementation on a Digitek Preview terminal. Included in the programs were functions for zooming, cropping, scaling, rotating, and editing a scanned bit map. Output on the Digitek phototypesetter was at a resolution of 667 dots per inch. Unlike the Linotype and Compugraphic (see 1985) logotype sub-systems which store characters in outline to enable treatment as a normal fount, the Itek system held the subject in bit map form only.

FES H. Berthold AG unveiled the M series of products at DRUPA. Nucleus of the system was a workstation founded on Sun Microsystems hardware embodying the Motorola 68020 microprocessor. Systems memory size was 4Mb. augmented by a 108Mb. Winchester disc. User interface consisted of a keyboard and mouse. An Ethernet interface was integral to the terminal allowing communication with a Data Tower file server. Pages with text and graphics were assembled interactively at the WYSIWYG display.

FES Compugraphic Corporation disclosed the MCS 6000 workstation for assembling pages with text and graphics. Almost inevitably the hardware emanated from Sun Microsystems and embodied a WYSIWYG screen where electronic cut-and-paste could take place. Direct connections to four PowerView terminals and/or MCS controllers were available. Text composition was effected on the MCS and PowerView equipment, the processed files being passed to the MCS 6000 workstation for page make-up. Graphics entered the system from the intelligent Scanner 2000 (see 1984). Once on the screen, the images could be cropped, rotated, and reversed.

GRA Two input scanners released by H. Berthold AG as part of the M series of products. For line drawings, logotypes, and the like, a Microtek scanner of 200 dots per inch resolution was provided. To cope with high-resolution linework and continuous-tone subjects, Berthold has developed its own HR Scanner employing CCD technology. From the HR Scanner a couple of output files could be obtained: a view file of low-resolution for display on a page make-up screen and an imaging file of high-resolution for output

FES Linotype Ltd. released a new APL-230 terminal incorporating a video screen with a black-on-white image, the characters appearing in Helvetica Medium. Within a month of the launch, the trade press reported accumulated sales of 250 units.

FES AM Varityper introduced a new 20/20 terminal to the EPICS typesetting system. It augmented the established batch composition and pagination facilities of the system with operational interactivity by integration of a large split-screen exhibiting true type styles in the WYSIWYG or job representational area of the display.

PTS Linotype was put up for sale by its parent company, the matter remaining unresolved at the end of 1986. It was not until April 1987 that Commerzbank AG purchased the business with a view to offering stock to the public on the Frankfurt exchange.

INDEX

A. B. Dick Co., 38, 71

Aachen (Brignall), 34

Aarhus Stiftsbogtrykkerei, 54

Accolade (Williams), 50

ACM 9000 phototypesetter, 44, 52

ACM 9001 phototypesetter, 44

Addressograph-Multigraph Corporation, 28, 29, 40, 44, 45, 50

Adobe Systems, 64, 70

Adsans (Tracy), 24

Advanced Imaging Software, 65

Advanced Typography Program (ATP/54). 54

AdVantage 5000 unit, 57

Agfa-Gevaert, 60, 61, 66

AH Development Syndicate Ltd., 13

Akzidenz Grotesk, 5

Albertus (Wolpe), 20

Aldine, 18

Aldus Corporation, 70

Aldus PageMaker software, 67

Aldus (Zapf), 13

Alfa System Partner, 73

All-Purpose Linotype machine, 18

Allen, George, 1

Allied Chemical Corporation, 57

Alpha (Bauer), 7

Alphacomp, 51

Alphanumeric Inc., 32, 38, 43

Alphanumeric Photocomposer System, 32

Alphatype Corporation, 42, 51, 55, 57, 59, 71

Alphatype CRS 4900 phototypesetter, 68

Alphatype CRS 9900 digital CRT phototypesetter, 65

Alphatype CRS phototypesetter, 55

Alphatype Multi-Set System, 69

Alphatype phototypesetting machine, 31

AM 707 phototypesetter, 40

AM 725 phototypesetter, 44

AM 744 phototypesetter, 44

AM 747 phototypesetter, 44

AM International, 38, 56, 58, 60, 61, 63, 68

AM Varityper, 62, 63, 65, 67, 68, 69, 70, 73, 75

Amalgatype, 10

American Bankers' Association, 29

American Type Founders Co., 2, 3, 4, 5, 9, 41, 42

Americana Annual, 29

Amsterdam Typefoundry, 32

Amtrol minicomputer, 46

APL-100 terminal, 61

APL-200 terminal, 61

APL-230 terminal, 75

Apollo (Frutiger), 30

Apple Computer, 61, 70, 73

Apple LaserWriter electronic printer, 70

Apple Lisa computer, 63, 70

Apple Macintosh computer, 67, 70

AppleTalk, 67, 70

APS-2 phototypesetter, 32, 38

APS-3 phototypesetter, 38

APS-4 phototypesetter, 44

APS-5 phototypesetter, 63, 64

APS-6 80/Laser phototypesetter, 70

APS-6 108/CRT phototypesetter, 70

APS-6 70/CRT phototypesetter, 70

APS-301 phototypesetter, 61

APS-313 phototypesetter, 61

APS-Microcomposer, 62

APSu5 phototypesetter, 59, 63, 64

Arabic script, 9, 10, 14, 24, 27

Aries (Gill), 23

Arrighi Italic (Warde), 22, 28, 29

Arts and Crafts Exhibition Society, 2

Ashendene Press, 15

ASME News, 18

Association of Correctors of the Press, 35

Asociation Typographique Internationale, 29, 48, 54, 55

Astronomical Ephemeris, 34

At the Sign of the Dolphin, London, 13

Atex Inc., 50, 57, 59, 60, 66

ATF Typesetter, 25, 30, 31, 42

August, Robert Carl, 13

Auriga (Carter), 33

Autokon 1000 laser scanner, 66, 68, 74

Autokon 8400 camera, 53

Autologic Inc., 43, 44, 59, 60, 62, 63, 64, 69, 70

Autologic/Bobst, 61

automatic line justification, 21

automatic self-quadding, 18

Automatic Type Machine, 6

Automix Keyboards Inc., 40, 49, 54, 57

Autoreader optical reader, 43, 47, 49

Avante Garde Gothic (Lubalin and Carnase), 42, 59

Ayer Award for Excellence in Newspaper Typography, 18

Bafour, Georges, 27

Bancroft, John Sellers, 4, 5

Barnett, Michael, 32

Barnhart Bros. & Spindler, 4

Barth, Hans, 1

Baryta paper, 16

Baskerville Cyrillic (Carter), 60

Baskerville Series 169, 15

Batelle Memorial Institute, 24

Bauer, Konrad F. (1903–1970), 7, 42

Bauer Giesserei typefoundry, 17, 20, 28, 44

Bauhaus, 16, 67

Baum, Walter, 7

Bawtree, Alfred E., 11

Bayer, Herbert (d. 1985), 16, 67

Bayer Type, 16

BBR patent, 27

Beaujon, Paul (pseudonym) *see* Warde, Beatrice

Bedford Computer Corporation, 56, 62

Behind the Magnesium Curtain, 28

Behrens, Peter, 3

Bell Gothic, 22

Bell Series 341, 18

Bell Telephone, 22

Bembo Series 270, 18

Benguiat, Ed, 42

Bennett, Paul (d. 1966), 36

Benton, Linn Boyd (*d.* 1932), 11, 19
Benton, M. F., 5, 42
Berthold (H.) AG, 5, 16, 26, 30, 34, 38, 46, 48, 52, 58, 59, 62, 71, 75
Berthold HR Recorder, 72
Berthold Laser Station, 72
Berthold Script (Lange), 48
Bestinfo, 65, 67, 69
Beta (Bauer), 7
Bibliographical Society, 3
Birdcage (Linotype Junior), 6
BitBlaster raster image processor, 64
BitCaster raster image processor, 64
BitPrinter machine, 64
BitSetter 3100 phototypesetter, 64
Bitstream Inc., 33, 59
Blakiston Company, 26
Blanchard, Andre, 27
Bloom, Dr. Otto, 16, 25
Blower Linotype, v, 1, 13
Blumenthal, Joseph, 36
Bobst Graphic Systems, 46, 47, 53, 55, 57, 59
Bodley Head, 32
Book Production War Economy Agreement, 23
Bouchery & Mincel, 40
Boyden, G. A., 6
Bradford Observer, 5
Bradley Jr., Morton C., 27
Breeze make-up terminal, 64
Breughel (Frutiger), 30
Brightype conversion system, 27
Brignall, Colin, 34
British Federation of Master Printers, 27
British Industries Fair (1953), 26
British National Bibliography, 31
British Printer, The, 2
British Typographers Guild, 17
British Typographia, 1
Broadbent, Walter, 14
Brock, Emma I., 30
Brown, F. H., 6
Brown, Thomas, 13–14, 16
Bullen, Henry Lewis, 9
Bunnell, Isaac S., 12
Bunyan (Gill), 23
Burns, Aaron, 42
Burrett, Edward, 17
button banks, exchangeable, 37

Caddex, 64
calculator, first electronic, 24
Caldwell, Dr. Samuel, 24, 25
Caledonia (Dwiggins), 28
Cambridge University Press, 15, 21
Camex Inc., 51, 53, 56, 57, 59, 64, 66
Camex SuperSetter, 64
Canon LBP-10 printer, 65
Canon LBP-CX printer, 63, 65, 72, 73
CAPS Ltd., 31
Carlson, Chester F., 23–24
Carnase, Tom, 42, 59
Carter, Harry (*d.* 1982), 60
Carter, Matthew, 33, 59

Cary, Melvin, 16
Caslon (H. W.) & Co. Ltd., 21
Caslon Series 128, 12
Cassell & Co. Ltd., London, 6
Caxton Type Foundry, Market Harborough, 5
Caxton (Usherwood), 39
CBS Laboratories, 35
CCI, Europe, 74
Centaur (Rogers), 23, 29
Centennial (Frutiger), 30
Central School of Arts & Crafts, London, 6
Central Unit 300, 74
Century, 11
CG2961 phototypesetter, 39, 41, 46
CG4961 phototypesetter, 39, 41, 46
CG7200 headlining machine, 39
CG8600 phototypesetter, 59
CG9600 phototypesetter, 71–72
Champion workstation, 74
Charles (Sir) Reed & Sons Ltd., 8
Chaucer (Prince), 15
Chelgraph Ltd., 66, 69, 72, 73
Chelgraph raster image processor, 72, 73
Cheltenham Press, 5
Cheltenham typeface, 5
Chicago Herald, 1
Chicago Tribune, 24
Chicago Type Foundry, 45
Chicago World Fair, 2
Chorus Data Systems, 67
Church, Dr. William, v
Cincinnati Type Foundry, 1
CIS Newsletter, 34
Clemens, Samuel L. (Mark Twain), 1
Clowes *see* William Clowes
clustered front-end composition system, 45
Cobden-Sanderson, T. J., 6
Cognitronics Inc., 47
cold-type composition, 31
Collected Poems 1934–1952, 33
Collins, publishers, 15
Coltec Data Systems, 58
Coltec P-501 video editing unit, 49–50
Columbia University, 9
Comenius (Zapf), 13
Commerzbank AG, 75
Commodore PET personal computer, 61
Comp/Edit 5810 phototypesetter, 56
Comp/Edit 5900 phototypesetter, 60
Comp/Edit 6200 phototypesetter, 67
Comp/Edit 6300 phototypesetter, 63
Comp/Edit 6400 phototypesetter, 61
Comp/Edit 6830 phototypesetter, 68
Comp/Edit CRT phototypesetters, 65
Comp/Set 500 phototypesetter 50–51, 52, 53, 55
Composer 1500 terminal, 52
Composer 15 video editing unit, 45
composing stick attachment, 19
Composition Information Services, 34
composition system, computer-controlled, 27
Composition Systems Inc., 39, 71
Compositype, 6

Comprite Ltd., 39
CompStar 150 and 190 phototypesetters, 43
CompuWriter, 44
CompuWriter International, 46
Compugraphic Corporation, 31, 32, 33, 37, 39, 41, 42, 44, 46, 48 *passim*
Compugraphic phototypesetters, 13
Compuscan 170 OCR, 45
Compuscan Alpha OCR, 49
Compuscan Inc., 53
Compustor, 51
Computaprint Ltd., 34
Computer Composition Inc., 51, 54, 63
Computer Peripheral Sciences, 71
Computer Peripherals and Typesetting, 39
computer-aided, 33
Computer-Aided-Typesetter (C/A/T), 57
computer-controlled composition system, 27
computer-controlled typesetting, 33
computer-to-plate, direct, 64
computers, 31, 32, 33, 34, 67
Computype, 51, 54
Comtec, 58
Concorde (Lange), 48
Congress of the Association Typographique Internationale, 54–55
Congress of the British Federation of Master Printers (1953), 27
Congress (Williams), 50
Continental Type Foundry, New York, 16
Converkal conversion system, 33
Copy Processing Systems, 65
Copytronic phototypesetter, 52
CorRecTerm M100 video editing unit, 45
Correct Keyboard Fingering: A System of Fingering the Linotype Keyboard for the Acquisition of Speed of Operating, 7
Corvinus (Reiner), 6
CoSprite, 45
Cossor CoSprite DIDS 402 video editing unit, 40
Coventry Gauge and Tool Co. Ltd., 25
Cox Typesetting Machine Company, 4
Coxhead, Ralph C. (d. 1951), 11, 19, 26
CP/M operating system, 60
CPS Front-End Composition System, 67, 71
Cranach Press, 23
Crosfield Electronics Ltd., 32, 33, 44, 47, 70, 71
CRT, 35, 38, 47, 49
CRTronic phototypesetter, 57, 58, 61, 68, 74
Crystal Goblet, The, 6
CText, 64, 67
Cuneiform Systems, 67, 71
Curwen Press, 15, 66

Daily Herald, 15
Daily News, New York, 29
Daily Telegraph, 24
Dante (Mardersteig), 15, 28
Daphnis (Tiemann), 26
Data General Nova computers, 45, 46, 47, 49, 51, 52
Data Recording Systems, 69

Data Tower file server, 75
Datek Systems Ltd., 58
de Goeij, Dr. H. J. A., 25
de Roos, S. H. (d. 1962), 32
De Vinne, Theodore Low (d. 1914), 11
Deberny, Alexandre, 15
Deberny & Peignot typefoundry, 15, 30, 46
Degenner, Heinrich, 9–10
DeLittle, R. D., 2
Delphian (Middleton), 19
Delta Data Telterm video editing screens, 45
De Neederlandsche Financier, 4
Derbyshire Times, 3
Dest Data Corporation, 53
Di Spigna, Antonio, 59
Diatext phototypesetter, 52
Diatronic optical system, 26, 38
Diatronic photo-matrix grid, 38
Diatronic S, 46
Diatype machine, 30
Die neue Typographie, 17
Digico Micro 16, 43
Digigraph scanner, 47
Digiset phototypesetters, 35, 38, 58
Digital Equipment Corporation, 35, 37, 39, 43, 48, 52, 56
digital founts, 39
Digital Type Systems Ltd., 70
Digitek 3000 phototypesetter, 67, 68
Digitek 5000 phototypesetter, 71
Digitek phototypesetters, 63, 74–75
Digitek Preview terminal, 73, 74–75
Directory Tape Processor, 32
Display Matrix Lending Library, 11
DLC-1000 Composer, 54, 55
Document Composition Facility, 66
Double Crown Club, 15
Doves Press, Hammersmith, 6, 15
Dr. Boger organisation, 52, 60
Dr.-Ing. Rudolf Hell, 35, 44, 47, 58, 65, 71
Drane, Douglas, 50
Dreyfus, John, 28
DRUPA, 32, 38, 61, 62, 71, 72, 73, 74, 75
DryGraphic, 58
Duncan, John, 32, 34, 43
Dunraven, Lord (1841–1926), 16
Duplex display matrices, 20
DuPont, 70, 74
Dutton, Arthur, 13
Dvorak, August, 19
Dwiggins, W. A. (d. 1956), 28
Dymo Graphic Systems, 52, 54, 57
Dymo Industries Inc., 44, 52, 54, 56

E13B founts, 29
Eastman Kodak Company, 3
Eckert, J. P., 24
Econosetter, 51
ECRM Autokon, 65
ECRM Autoreader, 45
ECRM Inc., 43, 47, 49, 53, 54, 56, 60, 63, 66, 68
ECRM PelBox laser recorder, 72

EditWriter 7500 phototypesetter, 55, 58
Egmont (de Roos), 32
Egyptienne (Frutiger), 30
Ehrhardt Series 453, 21
Ektamatic units, 36
Eldorado (Dwiggins), 28
Electrographic Corporation, 21
Electronic Integrator and Calculator
    (ENIAC), 24
electronic page make-up, 60
Electronic Retina Computing Reader, 36
ELF system, 56
Elihu the Musical Gnu, 30
Elliott 803 computer, 35
Elliott Automation Ltd., 35
Elrod, Benjamin S., 12
Elrod Lead and Rule Caster, 12, 13, 14, 18
Eltra Corporation, 57
Emery, Ted, 25
Encyclopaedia Britannica, 21
ENIAC, 24
Enschede en Zonen, 3
Eocom laser platemaker, 51
Eocom raster image processor, 62, 64
Epics text management system, 62, 69
Erasmus Mediaeval (de Roos), 32
Essay on Typography, 23
Esselte AB, 56, 57
Esselte Letraset, 70
Essex Chronicle Series Ltd., 38
Estienne, Ecole, 2
Estienne (Jones), 13
Ethernet, 62, 64, 74, 75
Eurocat phototypesetter, 46, 55
European American Graphics, 62
Eusebius (Middleton), 19
Evening Post, Chicago, 11
Evening Post, Reading, 35
Everyman's Library, 33
ExecuWriter phototypesetter, 51
Express & Star, Wolverhampton, 67
Express Newspaper Ltd., London, 14

Fairchild Graphic Equipment, 26, 30, 38
Fairchild Graphic Systems, 45
Fairchild TTS 440 System, 37
Falcon (Dwiggins), 28
Fann Street Foundry, 8
Ferguson, Arthur, 4
Ferranti, 73
Ferranti CS5 system, 45
Ferranti CS7 system, 45
Filmklischee GmbH, 34
filmsetting, 27
Financial News, 3
First Band Machine, 1
First Principles of Typography, 21
Fishenden, R. B., 22
Flach, Robert, 55
Flange (Usherwood), 39
Fleuron, The, 6
Flickerletter, 13
Flickertype, 13

Flinsch typefoundry, 20
floppy disc, 48
Florentine (Middleton), 19
Folio (Bauer), 7
Fontana (Mardersteig), 15
Fontenay (Flach), 55
Fortune (Bauer), 7
Forum Capitals (Goudy), 24
Foss, Hubert, 15
Fotolist system, 29, 31
Fotosetter, 32
Fototronic 480 phototypesetter, 34
Fototronic 600 phototypesetter, 41, 46
Fototronic 1200 phototypesetter, 39
Fototronic TxT phototypesetter, 42–43
Four-Tower Monotype, 3
Fournier Series 185, 16
Frederick Hepburn Company, 11
Friden, 25
Friedman, Samuel, 16, 25
Friese-Greene, William, 4
front-end processor, 48
Frutiger, Adrian, 30
Frutiger (Frutiger), 30
Fundamentals of Modern Composition, 55
Fundicion Tipografica Neufville, Barcelona, 44
Funk & Wagnalls, 30
Futura (Renner), 17

Galliard (Carter), 33
Garamond Series 156, 14, 29
Gardner, Arthur E., 34
GARF, 25
Garnett, David, 52
Garth, Bill (*d.* 1975), 24, 25, 31, 52
Gaul, Albro T., 27
GB Techniques, 70
GCI, 63
GEC, 10
GEC Exhibition, Milan, 41
Geddes, Hunter, 39
General Composing Company, 9–10
General Electric Company, 10
General Printing Ink Co., New York, 19–20
Genesis electronic printer, 65
Geneva Bible, The, 28
Georgian (Jones), 13
Gibson Brothers, Washington, 5
Gilbert-Stringer, H. J., 7
Gill, Eric (1882–1940), 6, 23, 28
Gill Sans (Gill), 19, 23
Girard & Cie, 15
Glasgow Corporation Printing Department, 28
Glasgow Herald, 27
Globe, The, 3
Gloucester (Monotype), 5
Godden, Rumer, 30
Goldberg, Hiram, 11
Golden (Prince), 15
Goodhue, Bertram, 5
Goudy, Frederic, (*d.* 1947), 24
Goudy Modern (Goudy), 24
Goudy Old Style (Goudy), 24

Government Printing Office, South Africa, 25
Government Printing Office, USA, 24, 37
Granjon (Jones), 13
Grant, John C., 10, 12
Graphatron phototypesetting machine, 31
Graphex Inc., 41
Graphic Arts Research Foundation (GARF), 25, 26
Graphic Page terminal, 64
Graphic Systems Inc., 43, 46, 52, 57, 73
Graphics Text Organiser Terminal, 70, 73
Graphis Bold (Usherwood), 39
Graphitel AC7020 phototypesetter, 73
Graphitel S.A., France, 73
Gray, Peter, 26
GRI-909 computer, 45
Griffo (Mardersteig), 15
Gropius, Walter, 16
GSA 789 digital CRT phototypesetter, 58
GSA Computer Typesetting System, 36
Gschwind, Erich, 53, 55
Guild of Printing Trades Executives, 26
Gurtler, Andre, 53, 55
Guttinger S.A., 52, 58

H. O. Bullard, New York, 29
Haas typefoundry, 28, 46
Haddon, Walter, 5
Hadego phototypesetting machine, 25, 27
Hadriano (Goudy), 24
Hallmark International, 13
Halske, 12
Hammond, James B. (d. 1913), 11
Handbook of Basic Microtechnique, 26
Handbook of Computer-Aided Composition, 58
Hanrahan, J. E., 6
Hanson, Ellis, 31
Harling, Robert, 21
Harris 1100 video editing unit, 43
Harris 2200 display system, 47–48, 56
Harris 2500 composition system, 48
Harris 7400 phototypesetter, 53
Harris 7600 phototypesetter, 53
Harris 8300 terminal, 64, 74
Harris Corporation, 42, 47, 53, 54, 60
Harris Graphics Ltd., 64
Harris-Intertype Corporation, 29, 41, 46
Harris-Seybold, 29
Hart, George Eaton, 17
Hart, Horace, 4
Harvard University Press, 14
Hastech PagePro system, 59, 60, 64, 70
Hattersley composing machine, v
Headliner 810 photolettering machine, 37
Heighlin Ltd., 59
Helga (Kleukens), 28
Helvetica (Miedinger), 28
Hendrix 3400 terminal, 48
Hendrix 5102FD video editing unit, 41, 45
Hendrix 5200 video editing unit, 45
Hendrix Electronics Inc., 41, 48, 49, 70
Hepburn Company, 19

Hewitt, Graily, 6
High-Speed Model C Intertype linecaster, 26
Higonnet, Rene A. (1902–1983), 7, 23, 26, 30, 31, 62
Higonnet-Moyroud phototypesetting machine, 24, 25, 27
Hilton, Robert, 2
History of the Nonesuch Press, The, 28
History of the Old English Letter Foundries, The, 3
HMSO, 40
Hodgkin, S. H. and P. E., 4
Hoe (R.) & Crabtree Ltd., 25
Hoell, Louis (d. 1935), 20
Holla (Koch), 20
Hollandsche Mediaeval (de Roos), 32
Honeywell, 40, 112
Horizon (Bauer), 7
Horman, Harold, 20
Huebner, William C., 23
Hughes, Alan, 39
Hughes Laboratory, Malibu, 31
Hunter, Edgar Kenneth, 13
Hydraquadder attachment, 29

IBM, 33, 36, 38, 41, 43, 48, 53, 60, 65, 66, 69
IBM 360 computer, 35 38
IBM 360/30 computer, 34
IBM 1100 computer, 35
IBM 1620 computer, 34
IBM 3820 electronic printer, 69
IBM 4250 printer, 61
IBM 6670 laser printer, 58
IBM Selectric Typewriter, 32
IBX phototypesetter, 72–73
Icone (Frutiger), 30
Ikarus (Karow), 50
Imagitex, 62, 68, 70
Imago (Lange), 48
Imhoff, Ernst, 70
Imlac Composer, 60
Imlac Corporation, 45, 52
Impressum (Bauer), 7
Imprimerie Nationale, 27
Imprint, The, 10
Index Medicus, 34
Information International Inc., 44, 47, 51, 57, 70
Initial Teaching Alphabet, 33
Inland Printer Company, 7
Inland Type Foundry, 4
Intel 8008 microprocessor, 51
Intelligent Machine Corporation, 27
Interleaf, 64
International Computers Ltd., 35–36
International Metals, 39
International Printing Exhibitions see IPEX
International Typeface Corporation, 42, 59, 70
International Typesetting Machine Company, 10, 12
International Typographers Union, 24
Interset, 66, 67
Intertype Corporation, 12, 23, 29, 31,

34, 39, 40
Intertype F mixer machine, 20
Intertype Fotomatic, 32
Intertype Fotosetter, 24, 26, 27, 28, 29
Intertype Ltd., UK, 13, 26
Intertype machines, 10, 11, 17, 18, 20, 36
Intertype Model F, 18, 21
Intertype Model G, 19, 21, 22
Intertype Model H, 19, 21
Intertype Monarch linecaster, 30, 33
Intran, 64, 67
Ionic, 15–16
IPEX (1904), 7
IPEX (1925), 16
IPEX (1936), 21
IPEX (1955), 28
Iridium (Frutiger), 30
Italic Quartet, 28
Itek Corporation, 53, 57–58, 59, 60, 61, 63, 65,
    67, 68, 69, 70
Itek Graphix Corporation, 70, 71, 73
Itek Large Systems Operations, 65

J. M. Dent Ltd., 33
Jackson, F. Ernest, 10
Jackson, Holbrook, 15
Jenson, Nicholas, 6
Jessen (Koch), 20
Joanna (Gill), 23
Johnson, A. F., 20
Johnson, Frank A., 4
Johnston, Edward (d. 1944), 6, 8, 10, 11, 23
Jones, George W., 1, 2, 13
Journal of Commerce, 11
Journal of Typographic Research, The, 37
Jubilee (Gill), 23, 24, 27
Justape computer, 37
Justotext, 41, 70
Justowriter system, 25, 30, 42

Kastenbein composing machine, v
Keeping Well, 16
Kelmscott Press, 2, 3, 15
Kennerley (Goudy), 24
Kessler, Count, 23
Key Corporation, 57
Keycomp input perforators, 40
Kimball, H. Ingalls, 5
Kindersley, David, 56
Kleukens, Christian (d. 1955), 28
Kleukens Antiqua, 28
Klingspor, Dr. Karl (d. 1950), 3, 25
Klingspor typefoundry, 20, 26, 28
Knuth, Donald, 57
Koch, Rudolph (d. 1934), 3, 20
Kodak, 36, 47, 59, 63
Kreiter Brothers, 45
Kurzweil Data Entry Machine (KDEM), 57
Kyte, Derek, 66

L & M News, 17
La Disfatta, 27
Lagerman, Alexander, 1

Lane, Sir Allen and Richard, 29
Lange, Gunter Gerhard, 48
Lanston Monotype Co., 1, 14, 17, 24, 42
Lanston Monotype Corporation, 5, 7, 10, 11,
    12, 18
Lanston, Tolbert (d. 1913), 1, 2, 3, 11
Lardent, Victor, 19
LaserWriter Plus electronic printer, 73, 74
Lasercomp, 54, 62, 65, 66
Lasercomp Blaser, 69
Lasercomp Express, 71
Lasercomp imaging engine, 64
Lasercomp Pioneer, 71
Lasercomp Sprint, 63
lasers, 31, 46, 54, 55
LaserScribe 8415 electronic printer, 69
Laserset phototypesetter, 61
Leamington (Williams), 50
Lectern Bible, 29
LED arrays, 61, 63
Leeds Mercury, 2
Legibility Group, 16
Legros, Lucien A., 10, 12
Letraset Ltd., 28, 31
Letters of Credit, 24
Lettre d'Or competition, 54–55
Libra (de Roos), 32
Limited Editions Club, New York, 18
Limited Fount Machine, 5
Linasec computer, 33, 34, 37
Linklater, Eric, 29
Linocomp 1 phototypesetter, 48
Linocomp 2 phototypesetter, 51, 55
Linofilm COL-28 phototypesetter, 37
Linofilm Europa phototypesetter, 42
Linofilm phototypesetter, 28, 29, 30, 31, 32, 36
Linofilm Quick phototypesetter, 34, 35, 38
Linofilm Super Quick phototypesetter, 39
Linofilm VIP phototypesetter, 42, 46, 51, 54
Linograph Corporation, 23
Linograph machine, 10, 14
Linograph Model 3, 13, 22, 50
Linolite magazines, 19
Linoscreen Composer terminal, 58, 65
Linoterm phototypesetter, 55
Linotron 101 phototypesetter, 63
Linotron 202 phototypesetter, 57, 58, 59, 61,
    68, 69
Linotron 303 phototypesetter, 49, 50, 60
Linotron 404 phototypesetter, 56–57
Linotron 505 phototypesetter, 38, 40, 49, 50
Linotron 505C phototypesetter, 43
Linotron 505TC phototypesetter, 47
Linotron 505-TC-100 phototypesetter, 49
Linotron 606 phototypesetter, 52, 56
Linotron 1010 phototypesetter, 35, 37
Linotronic phototypesetter, 53
Linotronic 100 phototypesetter, 67, 69, 70
Linotronic 300 phototypesetter, 65, 67, 69, 70,
    71, 73, 74
Linotronic 500 phototypesetter, 71, 73
Linotype & Machinery Ltd., 1, 7, 9, 13, 21, 27,
    30, 37, 64

Linotype Auto-Ejector, 23
Linotype Company Ltd., 2, 3, 5, 7, 8, 13
Linotype Elektron linecaster, 32, 37
Linotype Group of Companies, 4, 10, 17, 24, 25, 30, 33, 48, *passim*
Linotype Junior linecaster (Birdcage), 6
Linotype Ltd., 67, 75
Linotype machines, 9, 12, 14, 18, 20, 21, 22, 27, 36
Linotype Model 1 linecaster, v, 4, 11, 14, 15, 16, 17, 30
Linotype Model 4 linecaster, 8, 9, 10, 37
Linotype Model 4SM linecaster, 14, 37
Linotype Model 6SM linecaster, 16, 37
Linotype Model 48SM linecaster, 21
Linotype Model 70 linecaster, 30
Linotype Model 794 linecaster, 41
Linotype Model Fleet 54 linecaster, 27
Linotype Modern (Tracy), 24
Linotype Parts Co., New York, 15
Linotype System V, 50
Linotype-Paul Ltd., 38, 43, 46, 61, 63, 67
Linotype Users Association, 4
Listomatic sequential card camera system, 32
Lithomat Corporation, 24
Litton Industries, 63, 65, 67
Logicon Inc., 60
Logotype sub-system, 64, 68
London & North Eastern Railway, 19
London School of Printing, 25, 26, 27, 28, 29
London Society of Compositors, 27
London Typographical Society, 27, 33
Look! No Hands, 34
Los Angeles Times, 33
low-quadding device for Intertype machines, 20
Lowe, George Prescott, 27
Lowe and Brydone, 16, 22
LP 2300 laser plain paper proofing system, 73
LS210 phototypesetter, 65
LSP *see* London School of Printing
Lubalin, Herb (*d.* 1981), 42, 59
Lubalin Graph (Lubalin), 59
Ludlow, Washington I., 8
Ludlow Industries UK, 44
Ludlow machines, 9, 11, 12, 36
Ludlow Typograph Co., 8, 10, 12, 13, 19, 27, 29, 44
Ludwig & Mayer GmbH, 64
Lundy Electronics, 63
Lutetia (van Krimpen), 3
Lux Bildstudio GmbH, Frankfurt, 38
Lynton (Usherwood), 39

M.A.N., 22
M series terminals (H. Berthold AG), 75
McCorquodale & Co. Ltd., 29
Machinery Trust Ltd., 7
McIntosh, Ronald, 37, 38, 41, 46, 56, 61
Macintosh Plus computer (Apple), 73
Mackellar, Smiths & Jordan, 1
Macy, George, 18
Magic system (H. Berthold AG), 62
Magnaset 226 phototypesetter, 44, 47

magnetic core memory, 27
Magnetic Ink Character Recognition (MICR), 29
Magnetic Tape Selectric Composer, 36
Magnetic Tape Selectric Typewriter, 33–34
Magpie graphic workstation, 66
MagSet record/playback system, 48
Maiman, Theodore H., 31
Malin, Charles (*d.* 1956), 28
Maltron I keyboard, 43
Maltron II keyboard, 54
Manchester Guardian, 5
Manutius, Aldus, 15
Marathon (Koch), 20
Mardersteig, Giovanni (1892–1977), 3, 15, 28, 55
Margerison, Dr. Tom, 35
Mark VIII CRT phototypesetter, 58
Mark IX CRT phototypesetter, 67
Maryland Composition Company, 52
Mason, J. H., 10
Massachusetts Institute of Technology, 24, 25, 32
Matrotype Ltd., 34, 45
Matura (Reiner), 6
Maunchly, J. W., 24
Maxi system (Automix), 54
Maximilian Antiqua (Koch), 20
Maximus (Tracy), 24
MCS 100 controller, 65, 74
MCS 6000 workstation, 75
MCS 8000 digital CRT phototypesetter, 67
MCS 8200 phototypesetter, 60
MCS 8400 digital CRT phototypesetter, 60, 68
MCS 8600 digital CRT phototypesetter, 63, 65
MDT 350 terminal, 56
Mechanism of the Linotype, The, 7
Media (Gurtler, Mengelt, Gschwind), 53
Media Industry, 41
Media Unit, 61
Meidinger, Max, 28
Melior (Zapf), 13
Mendel, Vera, 52
Mengelt, Christian, 53, 55
Mercurius (Reiner), 6
Mergenthaler Printing Company, 1
Mergenthaler, Ottmar (*d.* 1899), v, 1, 2–3, 5, 13
Mergenthaler Linotype Co., 2, 6, 12, 13, 15, 22, 28, 35, 36–37, 41, 45, 58
Mergenthaler Linotype GmbH, 42, 53, 57, 67
Mergenthaler Setzmaschinenfabrik GmbH, 4, 6
Meridian (Reiner), 6
Meridien (Frutiger), 30
Merrymount Press, 14
Messenger Group of Newspapers, 63
Meteor terminals, 62
Meteora (Sutter), 55
Metro (Dwiggins), 28
Metropolitan Museum of New York, 11, 29
Metroreader OCR, 52
Metteur machine (Uhertype), 22
Meynell, Gerard, 10

Meynell, Sir Francis (1891–1975), 3, 12, 52
MGD Graphic Systems Division, Rockwell
    International, 47, 52, 56, 57
MGD Metro-Set phototypesetter, 52, 58
Miami Herald, 34
Mickey Mouse linecaster, 15
MICR, 29
Microcomposer II front-end system, 69
Microdata 810 minicomputer, 42
Microsoft Word, 69
Microtek scanner, 74, 75
Middleton, Robert Hunter, 19
Miles 33, 54, 58, 60, 66
Miller & Richard typefoundry, 26
Minerva (Stone), 27
Minitek front-end system, 67
MIT *see* Massachusetts Institute of Technology
Model 3800 electronic printer, 53
Model 48 linecaster (Linotype), 21
Model 48SM linecaster (Linotype), 21
Model 50 linecaster (Linotype), 21
Model 50SM linecaster (Linotype), 21
Model 6 linecaster (Linotype), 20
Model 903 computer (Elliott), 35
Modern and Historical Typography, 29
Modern Printing, 8
Modular Composition System (MCS), 60, 63,
    65, 68
Mondadori, Verona, 25, 27
Monoline composing machine, 3, 10
Monophoto Filmsetter, 21, 26, 27, 29, 33,
    34, 36
Monophoto Filmsetter Mark 3, 34
Monophoto Filmsetter Mark 4, 37, 40
Monophoto 400/8 phototypesetter, 51
Monophoto 400/31 phototypesetter, 49, 51
Monophoto 600 phototypesetter, 41
Monotype 512 phototypesetter, 71
Monotype Casters, 8, 9, 10, 11, 13, 15, 19,
    33, 41
Monotype Casters and Typefounders Society, 2
Monotype Corporation Ltd., 3, 14, 18, 28, 36,
    41, 48, 49, 60, 70, 73
Monotype Duplex Keyboard, 9
Monotype Electronic Perforator, 37
Monotype Giant Caster, 16
Monotype International, 54, 65, 69, 71
Monotype machines, 10, 29
Monotype Material Maker, 14
Monotype Model D Keyboard, 8–9, 37
Monotype Paper Tape Conversion Unit, 35
Monotype Photolettering Machine, 33
Monotype Recorder, The, 6, 7
Monotype Studio-lettering machine, 40
Monotype Super Caster, 17, 36
Monotype System 272 video input keyboard, 60
Monotype Triangle machine, 2
Monotype Users Association, 11
Moran, James, 56
Morey, Walter W., 16
Morisawa, 58
Morison, Stanley (1889–1967), 2, 12, 14, 15,
    19, 21, 23, 28, 37

Morris, William (1834–1896), 2, 3, 5, 15
Motorola 68000 microprocessor, 62, 69, 74
Motorola 68020 microprocessor, 72, 73, 74
Moyroud, Louis, 7, 23, 26, 30, 31, 55, 73
MTSC (IBM), 36
MTST (IBM), 33
Muirhead & Co. Ltd., 39
Muirhead Data Communications, 71
Mulholland, Brian, 66
multiplexors, 35
Multiset composition system, 57, 111
Murray, Donald, 6
Muset special-purpose typesetting computer, 39
MVP editing terminal, 54, 55
Mycro-Comp 1100-Plus composition system, 74
Mycro-Comp 550 composition system, 74
Mycro-Comp composition system, 54
Mycro-Tek, 54, 58, 64, 74

National Compositype Company, Baltimore, 9
National Geographic magazine, 31
National Graphical Association (NGA), 33, 35,
    60, 71
National Library of Medicine, Bethesda, 34
National Typographic Company, 1
Nautical Almanac Office, 34
Nebitype matrices, 36
Neue Haas-Grotesk (Miedinger), 28
Neuland (Koch), 20
New Testament in Cadenced Form, The, 27
New York Times, 12
New York Tribune, 1
Newcastle Evening Chronicle, 3
Newcastle University, 32, 43
News Index, 17
News International, 71
Newspaper Design Annual Award (1954), 27
Newspaper Electronics Corporation, 52
Newspaper Systems Development Group,
    48, 54
Nixie tubes, 40
Nonesuch Press, 52
Norsk Data, 58
Norton, Robert, 70
Nottingham Evening Post, 56
Nuernberger, Philip, 8
NV Exploitatiemaatschappij, Amsterdam, 25
NV Quod Bonum, Haarlem, 25

OCR 1 system, 49
OCR techniques, 36
OCR-B (Frutiger), 30
Offenbach (Koch), 20
Office Equipment Manufacturers Assoc., 29
Officina Bodoni, 15
Offizin (Tiemann), 26
Offset Processes, 37
offset-lithography, 29
Ogden, Ashley, 20
Old Style No. 2, 15
Olivetti M24 personal computer, 71
Olympian (Carter), 33
Omega (Kleukens), 28

Omnitech 2000 phototypesetter, 57–58
Omnitech 2100 phototypesetter, 60
Omnitext terminals, 47, 52
Ondine (Frutiger), 30
ONE composition systems, 52, 60, 74
optical character escapement carriage, 25
optical scanner, 27
Optima (Zapf), 13
Oriani, Alfredo, 27
Orion (Zapf), 13
Orotype machine, 1, 17, 22
Orpheus (Tiemann), 26
Orrell, Andrew, 13–14, 16
Ottmar Mergenthaler & Co., 1
Overseen, Netherlands, 25
Oxford University Press, 29

P-400 electronic printer (Agfa), 61
Pabst Roman (Goudy), 24
Pacesetter optical system, 44
PageMaker software, 70
PageMaster video make-up terminal, 62
PagePlanner system, 64, 69
PageView terminal, 53
Pagitek equipment, 59
Paige, J. W., 1
Paige Compositor, 1
Palatino (Zapf), 13
Parker, Mike, 33, 59
Partners in Progress, 31
Patriot Ledger, 27
Paul, Klaus (d. 1985), 66–67
PDP-8 computer, 35, 37, 39, 44, 49, 52
PDP-8E computer, 43
PDP-11 computer, 39, 43, 48, 50, 54, 56
PDP-11/35 computer, 53
PDS-1 computer, 45, 52
PE9000 recorder, 73
Peery, Walter, 24, 26, 41
Peery Photographic Typecomposing System, 26
Peignot, Gustave, 15
PelBox laser recorder, 68, 72
Pelican Press, 12
Penguin Books, 29, 50, 66
Penrose Annual, The, 13, 16, 21, 22, 26, 34
Penta Systems, 39, 52, 54, 58, 62
Pentavision terminal, 62
Pepita (Reiner), 6
Perpetua (Gill), 23, 28
Perq workstation, 64, 70
Perry Publications Inc., 32–33, 36
Perry typefount, 49
Personal Composition System, 63
Personal Typesetting Workstation, 69, 73
Personal Typography System, 73–74
Peterson, Hans, 10
Phillips, Arthur, 39, 58
Phoebus (Frutiger), 30
photo-matrices, 29
Photo-Composition and Make-Up by
   the Rotofoto Process, 26
Photo-Lettering Inc., New York, 21
photo-matrix disc, 30, 46

photo-matrix film strips, 35
Photo-Typesetting: a description of the
   Rotofoto System, 24
Photocomp, 20, 41
photocomposing, 16
photographic composing machine, 13
photographic Ludlow, 25
photolettering machine, 12, 20
Photoline, 13
Photomix phototypesetters, 52
Photomix 8000 phototypesetter, 43, 46, 49, 70
Photomix 8400 phototypesetter, 49
Photon 200 phototypesetter, 28–29, 30, 32
Photon 540 phototypesetter, 32
Photon 550 phototypesetter, 35
Photon 560 phototypesetter, 46
Photon 713 phototypesetter, 35
Photon 713-5 phototypesetter, 38
Photon 713-10 phototypesetter, 38
Photon 713-20 phototypesetter, 36
Photon 713-100-15 phototypesetter, 40
Photon 713-200-15 phototypesetter, 40
Photon Compositor, 46, 51
Photon Fontmaster 532 phototypesetter, 40
Photon Inc., 26, 30, 31, 32, 36–37, 38, 40, 42,
   46, 50, 51, 52, 58
Photon machines, 25, 27
Photon Pacesetter phototypesetter, 41, 44
Photon Pacesetter (Marks 2, 3, 4) 46, 49, 51
Photon ZIP phototypesetter, 31, 34
Photoprint Plates Ltd., Essex, 29
photosetting, 29
phototypesetting, 18
Phototypositor display photolettering
   machine, 31
Pica Machine (linecaster), 7
Pick, Frank, 11
Pierpont, Frank H., 11
Pitman, Sir James, 33
Plantin modernised, 19
Plantin Series 110, 11
Plumet, 22
Plus Printing Metals, 57
PM Filmsetter 1001, 38
Poliphilus Series 170, 15
Porszolt, E., 4
Portsmouth & Sunderland Newspapers Ltd., 40
PostScript page description language, 64
power-assisted shifting of matrix magazines, 19
PowerPage software, 63, 65
PowerView terminals, 75
PowerView 5 terminal, 73
PowerView 10 terminal, 65, 69, 73
Practice of Typography, The, 11
Press Computer Systems, 50, 67
Price, Pershke, 31
Prime 100 computer, 49, 50
Prince, Edward (d. 1923), 6, 15
PRINT 68 exhibition, 39
PRINT 74 exhibition, 51
PRINT 85 exhibition, 67, 69
Print in Britain, 27
Printers Ornaments, 23

Printing, Packaging and Allied Trades Research
    Association, 24
Printing Design and Layout, 20
Printing Exhibition, London (1925), 16
Printing Managers' Trade Society, 27
Printing Review, 27
Printing Types, 14
Printing World, 27
Prisma (Koch), 20
Private Angelo, 29
Protext 2000 composition system, 66, 74
PSS Peripherals, 63
PTS 2000 phototypesetter, 26
PTS 8000 phototypesetter, 38
Pulsometer Engineering Company, 4
punchcutting machine, 19
Purdy, Peter, 37, 38, 41, 46, 56, 61
Purup Electronics, 73

quadding, automatic and centring, 21
Quadex Corporation, 53, 57
Quadritek 1200 terminal, 53, 59
Quadritek phototypesetter, 60
Quadritek terminals, 61
Qubix, 64

Radiant (Middleton), 19
Raithby, Lawrence & Co., 2
Raleigh (Williams), 50
raster image processor, 70
Ratio Roman (Kleukens), 28
Raycomp 100 graphic terminal, 51, 56
Raymond, Francois, 27
Raystar phototypesetter, 61
Raytheon Co., 60
RCA 301 computer, 33
RCA, 35, 44, 47, 51
Reade, William, 8, 9
Real Time Composition System, 56
Recessed Linotype slug, 8
Recognition Equipment Inc., 36
Record Gothic (Middleton), 19
Reed, Talbot Baines (d. 1892), 3
Reed (Sir Charles) & Sons Ltd., 3
Reese, Max, 27
Reiner, Imre, 6, 21, 29
Reinhardt & Co. Inc., 26–27
Renner, Paul (d. 1956), 17
Rettig, George, 8
Revue (Brignall), 34
Richard Clay Ltd., 34
Richards, 6
Ricoh 4080 electronic printer, 65
Robertson, John, 13–14, 16
Rocappi Inc., 33
Rockwell International, 47, 58
Rogers, Bruce (d. 1957), 23, 29
Rogers, John R. (d. 1934), 2, 20
Romanee (van Krimpen), 3
Romic (Brignall), 34
Romulus (van Krimpen), 3
Rondthaler, Ed, 20, 21, 42
Rotary Matrix Machine, 1

Rotofoto, 25
Rotofoto Proof Projector, 25
Rotofoto system, 21, 24, 26, 27, 28, 29
Royal College of Art, 6
Royal Designer for Industry Award, 24
Royce Data Systems, 60, 66, 67
RT/PC workstation, 74
Rudhard typefoundry, 3
Rule Caster, 11
rule-form matrices, special, 19
*Rules for Compositors and Readers at the
    University Press, Oxford*, 4
Rutherford Machinery Division, 20
Rutherford Photo-Letter Composing
    Machine, 21

Sabon (Tschichold), 50
St. Bride Printing Library, 3
St. Clements Press, 17
St. John, R. H., 2
SAM (Sets All Matrices) hot-metal system,
    13, 36
Saskia (Tschichold), 50
Sasmats Ltd., 44
Satellite of the Sun, 30
Saul Brothers, Chicago, 12
Scandata 100 Data Management System, 66
Scangraphic Dr. Boger, 64, 65, 66, 72
Scanner 1000 system, 68
Scanner 2000 system, 65, 75
Scantext 1000 system, 60, 72
Scantext 2000 system, 72
Scantext phototypesetter, 64, 65
Schmoller, Hans (d. 1985), 66
Schuckers, J. W., 3
Scitex, 59, 61, 67
Scotch Roman, 27
Scotchprint, 32
Scotsman, The, 20
Scriptura (Kleukens), 28
Scudder, Wilbur, 3
Seaco 1600 phototypesetter, 44–45
Seagull (Williams), 50
Second Band Machine, 1
Series 100 system, 67
Serif Gothic (Lubalin), 59
Serifa (Frutiger), 30
Seybold, John W., 44, 55
Seybold Report, The, 44
Shaffstall Corporation, 54
Shah, Eddy, 63
Shakespeare and the Welfare State, 27
Shenval Press, Hertford, 21
Siemens AG, 44
Signa (Gurtler, Mengelt, Gschwind), 55
Signature, 21
Silcock, E., 26
Sim-X Pagescan, 62
Simon, Oliver, 15, 21
Simons, Hannah, 30
Simplex (de Roos), 32
Simplex One-Man Typesetter, 5, 6
Singer Graphic Systems, 41, 46

Singer Manufacturing Co., 25, 41, 43, 49, 52
Skipping Island, 30
Smith, H. O., 25, 26, 27
Smothers, R. J., 16
Society of Graphical and Allied Trades, 71, 82
Society of Industrial Artists and Designers, 18
Society of Lithographic Artists, Engravers,
    and Process Workers (SLADE), 60
Society of Typographic Arts, Chicago, 17
Society of Typographic Designers, 17
Solus (Gill), 23
Southward, John, 8
Southwark Offset Ltd., 40
Souvenir (Benguiat), 42
*Specification for Metric Typographic
    Measurement,* 47
Spectrum (van Krimpen), 3
Spilhaus, Athelstan F., 30
Spirascan, 56
Square-Base Model 1 Linotype, 2, 3
Staatliche Akademie der Graphischen Kunste,
    Leipzig, 26
Standard International Dictionary, 30
Standard-Union, 2
Star 8010 video workstation, 60
Star Parts Co., 15, 43, 44, 52
Star-Base Linotype Model 1, 3, 15
Staromat photolettering machine, 34
Starsettograph headlining machine, 34
STaRT newspaper composition system, 53
Stationers' Hall, 29
Steer, Vincent, 17, 20
Stellar (Middleton), 19
Stempel, David, 4
Stempel (D.) AG, 6, 13, 28, 67
Stephenson, Blake & Co. Ltd., 7, 8, 9, 15,
    21–22
Stephenson, Sir H. (*d.* 1904), 7
Stone, Reynolds (1909–1979), 27, 57
Story of Holly and Ivy, The, 30
Stradivarius (Reiner), 6
strike-on composition, 37
Stringertype machine, 7
Subiaco type, 15
Sun Chemical Co., 47, 52
Sun Microsystems, 74, 75
Suncom front-end system, 52
Sundwall, Joe, 59
Sunsetter phototypesetter, 47, 52
Super Caster, 14
super-display magazine for Linotype
    machine, 20
Super-Range linecaster, 21
SuperPage software, 69
SuperSetter system, 66
Superstar device, 34
Survival of Baskerville's Punches, The, 28
Sutter, Walter, 55
Swiss Locomotive and Machine Works,
    Winterthur, 22
System 7600, 54
System Integrators Inc., 64, 66, 70
System V, 53

System/25, 70

Tachytype machine, 4
Tansel, 31
tape-allotting system, 31
Taunton Telephone Directory, 32
Tegra, 65
Teletypesetter Corporation, 17, 30
Teletypesetter Multiface Perforator, 17, 30
Teletypesetter (TTS), 19, 26, 32
Tempo (Middleton), 19
Terminal 300 CR Terminal, 73
Texet Corporation, 62
Text Talking Terminal, 66
The Fleuron: a Journal of Typography, 15, 21
The Imprint magazine, 23
Thermo-Blo mould cooler, 22
*This Thing Called Rotofoto: some notes
    for young inventors,* 26
Thomas, Dylan, 33
Thompson, John S. (*d.* 1955), 7, 9, 27
Thompson Type Caster, 9, 10
Thompson Type Machine Co., Chicago, 9,
    12, 17
Thomson Computerset System, 35
Thomson Organisation, 35
Thorne Typesetting Machine Company, 4
Tiemann, Walter (*d.* 1951), 3, 26
Tiemann Mediaeval, 26
Time Inc., 26
Times, The, 19, 24
Times Europa (Tracy), 24, 46
Times Literary Supplement, The, 23, 31
Times New Roman (Morison), 15, 19
Times Union Building, New York, 17
Timmis, Walter S., 7
TPG exhibition (1965), 35
Tracy, Walter, 24, 46
trades unions, demarcation agreements, 30
Transito (Tschichold), 50
Tribune Book of Open Air Sports, The, 1
Troy type, 15
Tschichold, Jan (1902–1974), 7, 17, 19, 50
TTS tape operation, 17, 20, 30
Turnbull, Andrew, 32
Twain, Mark *see* Clemens, Samuel L.
Two-in-One Linotype machine, 18
two-letter matrices introduced, 21
Typary & Typon Company Ltd., 16
Typary machine, 1, 16, 22
type, leadless, 27
Type Designs: their History and Development,
    20
Type Plus, 68
Typecraft Systems Ltd., 61
Typefounders' Society, 2
Typeset-11, 48
Typesetters Inc., 39
Typesetting Methods: Old and New, 22
Typesettra, Toronto, 39
Typodyne phototypesetters, 41
Typograph linecasting machine, 2, 6, 9, 13
Typographical Association, 33

Typographical Printing Surfaces: the Technology and Mechanism of their Production, 12
Typography, 12, 21
Typophiles, The, 19, 36
Typotheter, 1

Uher, Edmund, 18
Uhertype phototypesetting system, 19, 21, 22, 50
Ullman, Dr. Max, 22
Ullman (J.) GmbH, Zwickau, 22
UltraComp input and editing equipment, 49
Unibus, 43
Unified Composer, 51
Unisetter phototypesetter, 52
unit-cut matrices, 26
unit-shift attachment, 33
United Printing Machinery Company, Baltimore, 6
United States Type Founders' Association, 1
Unitex, 65, 67
Unitype Company, 4
Unitype composing machine, 5
Univers (Frutiger), 28, 30
Universal Adjustable Mould, 5
Universal Ejector Blade, 9
Universal Knife Block, 9, 20
Universal Perforator, 32
Universal I phototypesetter, 46
Universal II phototypesetter, 46
Universal IV phototypesetter, 52
Universal Type Caster, 8, 12
Updike, Daniel B. (*d.* 1942)
Usherwood, Leslie, 39
Utex, Europe, 67
UX Imagesetter, 69

van Krimpen, Jan (*d.* 1958), 3
Varian 520 computer, 42
Varicomp 2000 system, 47, 51
Varicomp 2100 system, 51
Varicomp 3000 system, 47
varigear attachment, 33, 36
Varisystems Corporation, 47, 50, 51, 57, 62
Varisystems P16 minicomputer, 44, 46
Varityper 1010 strike-on system, 39
Varityper 720 system, 36
Varityper Division, Addressograph-Multigraph Corporation, 29, 31, 38
Varityper Headliner Photo-Composing Machine, 26, 28
Varityper strike-on machines, 19, 21, 24, 56, 70
VAX computer, 39
VAX-11/780 computer, 56
Venezia (Jones), 13
Verbal Technologies Inc., 66
Vernon, Alfred, 17
Versailles (Frutiger), 30
Victorline composing machine, 9–10
Video (Carter), 33
Videocomp 500 phototypesetter, 44, 51
Videocomp phototypesetter, 35, 47

Videojet 960 non-impact printer, 38
Videosetter 2414 phototypesetter, 49, 51
Videosetter Universal phototypesetter, 53
Vienna agreement, 59
Vienna Agreement for the Protection of Type Faces and their International Deposit, 48
Viewtech, 64, 66, 67, 70–71
Viewtex page dummying system, 67
Village Press, 24
Visible Language, 37
Visual Graphics Corporation, 31
Vox, Maximilien (1894–1974), 4, 50

Wakefield Chronicle, 4
Walbaum Series 374, 20
Waldorf Astoria Hotel, New York, 25
Walker, Sir Emery (*d.* 1933), 2, 6, 18, 19
Wallau (Koch), 20
Wang, Dr. An, 27
Wang Laboratories Inc., 57
Wapping, move to, 71
Warde, Beatrice (1900–1969), 6, 40
Warde, Frederic (*d.* 1939), 22–23, 28, 29
Waterlow & Sons Ltd., Dunstable, 22
Weiss, Emil R. (*d.* 1942), 23
Weiss Roman, 23
Weiss Rundgotisch, 23
Westover, George, 21, 26, 28, 29
Wheatley, Bill, 70
Whittaker (M. H.) & Sons Ltd., 13, 15, 17, 36, 64
William Clowes & Sons Ltd., 32
Williams, Adrian, 50
Winchester (Stephenson Blake), 5
Wiseman, Neil, 56
Wolpe, Berthold, 20
Wonderful World of Insects, The, 26–27
word processing, 34
Work of Jan Van Krimpen, The, 28
Works of Geoffrey Chaucer, The, 3
World Intellectual Property Organisation, 48
Writing and Illuminating and Lettering, 8
Wrolstad, Merald E., 37
Wyman & Sons Ltd., London, 5
Wynkyn de Worde Society, 29

Xenotron Ltd., 54, 60, 62, 63, 69, 71
Xenotron UX Imagesetter, 74
Xenotron Video Composer, 54, 56, 58
Xerox Corporation, 59, 60, 61
Xerox 2700 laser printer, 61, 64, 65
Xerox 3700 laser printer, 69
Xerox 5700 laser printer, 59
Xerox 8700 laser printer, 61
Xerox 9700 laser printer, 55
Xerox Publishing System, 66, 70
Xicon Data Entry, 49
Xylogics Inc., 45, 54, 65
Xyvision Inc., 62, 66, 70, 74

Ying, Richard, 50
Yorkshire Post Newspapers, 39

Zapf, Hermann, 13
Zapf Chancery, 13
Zapf International, 13
Zeno (Mardersteig), 15
Zilog Z80 chip, 69
Zilver Type (de Roos), 32